ABOUT *SCROOGENOMICS*

CHRISTMAS is a time of seasonal cheer, family get-togethers, holiday parties, and… gift giving. Lots and lots—and lots—of gift giving. But how many of us get gifts we like? How many of us give gifts not knowing what recipients want? *Scroogenomics* illustrates how our consumer spending generates vast amounts of economic waste—to the shocking tune of eighty-five billion dollars each winter, much of it financed by credit cards. Economist Joel Waldfogel shows us why it's time to stop the madness and think twice before buying gifts for the holidays.

When we buy for ourselves, every dollar we spend produces at least a dollar in satisfaction. Gift giving is different. We make less-informed choices and leave recipients less than satisfied, creating what economists call a "deadweight loss." This waste isn't confined to Americans— most major economies share in this orgy of wealth destruction. But by reprioritizing our gift-giving habits, *Scroogenomics* proves that we can still maintain the economy without gouging our wallets, and reclaim the true spirit of the holiday season.

scroogenomics

Princeton and Oxford
Princeton University Press

scroogenomics

WHY YOU SHOULDN'T BUY
PRESENTS FOR THE HOLIDAYS

JOEL WALDFOGEL

Copyright © 2009 by Princeton University Press

Published by Princeton University Press, 41 William Street, Princeton, New Jersey 08540

In the United Kingdom: Princeton University Press, 6 Oxford Street, Woodstock, Oxfordshire OX20 1TW

Library of Congress Cataloging-in-Publication Data

Waldfogel, Joel, 1962–

Scroogenomics : why you shouldn't buy presents for the holidays / Joel Waldfogel.

p. cm.

Includes bibliographical references and index.

ISBN 978-0-691-14264-7 (hardcover : alk. paper)   1. Consumption (Economics)   2. Gifts.   I. Title.

HB801.W272 2009

339.4'7—dc22

2009006177

British Library Cataloging-in-Publication Data is available

This book has been composed in ITC New Baskerville Std and New Caledonia LT Std

Printed on acid-free paper. ∞

press.princeton.edu

Printed in the United States of America

1 3 5 7 9 10 8 6 4 2

CONTENTS

Preface

I first encountered Christmas after my formal in-
doctrination as an economist. Where others see
hearthside scenes of sharing, I also saw—through
the eyes of an economist—a large and organized
institution for value destruction, hiding in plain
sight but obscured for most people by their warm
childhood memories.

I responded as any social scientist would. I
started doing research. I surveyed my students
about how much the gifts they received were
worth to them, as well as how much the givers
had paid. What I found is no surprise from the
standpoint of economic theory: gifts—things that
others buy for you—are poorly matched with your
preferences. As an institution for "allocating resources" (getting stuff to the right people), holiday giving is a complete loser. I wrote a little
paper in 1993 called "The Deadweight Loss of
Christmas" that set off a few alarms. Although I
have a day job teaching and doing research on serious topics in economics, I have long indulged a

habit of Yuletide research. A few years back I did some popular writing for *Slate,* and I found that I enjoyed communicating about research in ways that readers might find both informative and entertaining. What follows is my attempt to share my work on Yuletide economics with a broad audience.

I am grateful to my wife, Mary Benner, for supporting all of my endeavors, wacky or otherwise. I also thank Mary and her family for introducing me to Christmas but not disowning me despite the apparent fact that I am the most ungrateful son-in-law on the planet. I thank my father, Melvin, and my late mother, Gertrude, for raising me to deplore waste. Finally, I thank my children, Hannah and Sarah, for teaching me many things and, in particular, for their enthusiasm about the ideas for encouraging charitable giving at the holidays.

I wish you happy—and efficient—holidays.

scroogenomics

CHAPTER ONE

Introduction

Every December brings the same nightmarish vision. It begins at a deserted mall stacked with a million dollars' worth of products. Customers form a perimeter a thousand feet outside the mall. Then, out of nowhere, a red tornado strikes—just the mall and not the crowd—and lifts the clothing and appliances and books and DVDs into the air. As quickly as the cyclone landed, it rises back up to the sky. Then the products rain gently down on the crowd.

"Hey, I got a toaster," says someone in the crowd.

"Look, I got a red sweater, not my size or color," says another.

"Wow, I got a singing fish."

And these are the lucky ones.

Miraculously, no one is hurt, everyone gets something, and neither the building nor any of the products are damaged. But after the thrill of free stuff wears off, people realize that they do not have what they want.

I go around with a clipboard asking people in the crowd how much they would willingly have paid for what they got. A few got things they wanted, or now realize they want after reading the packaging. But most are unenthusiastic about their windfalls. They would not have been willing to pay anything close to the purchase price, if anything at all. When I tally the responses, people are willing to pay an average of twenty-five cents on the dollar of retail price.

I'd like to say you can rest easy because these events never happened. But they did, and they do every year in much of the world. The red tornado is Santa Claus. And despite the warm feelings he evokes in children, his tornado of giving does a perennially poor job of matching stuff with people. In so doing, he destroys a lot of value, just as he turned our million dollars' worth of products into a mere $250 thousand worth of satisfaction for the shoppers encircling the mall.

Every holiday season in the living rooms of families in rich countries we experience something similar to the red tornado, only without the actual funnel cloud. For months before the big day, mothers and fathers—mothers, mostly—run around trying to find the right gifts for their loved ones, young and old. Some gift recipients are easy to second-guess. It takes little imagination to predict that a four-year-old will like a doll or a toy truck. As kids get older, it gets tougher to find a surprise gift that they'll appreciate, but older kids often take out the guesswork with specific requests for this year's fashionably conformist clothes. And then there are the adults for whom we are obliged to get something. We know that Uncle Jim and his wife and kids will be there, so we have to get him something. But what sort of music does your nephew like this year? Does his tongue piercing provide a clue? And grandma's coming. You have no idea what she wants, but—believe me—she has even less of a clue about what you and your kids over seven want.

When the day arrives, families—and extended families—gather around a tree or a hearth or a menorah to exchange holiday gifts. Kids squeal in delight as they open their dolls and trucks. With young children especially, the gifts matter less than the ritual of ripping off wrapping paper and bows. Teenagers feign surprise—for grandma's benefit—and register actual approval for the gifts they specifically requested. They roll their eyes at the music and movies you buy them. Because you've raised them well, they manage a smile for grandma's gifts. What kid doesn't need a candle? But the fabricated smiles aren't limited to the teens. The adults all arrange their faces into expressions of pleasure as they unwrap items they would never buy for themselves. "A cribbage board? You shouldn't have," we tell our mothers-in-law. Indeed.

Christmas provides the occasion for a large amount of spending in predominantly Christian developed countries. In the United States, for example, retail sales during the month of December tower visibly over the volume in adjacent months. In some categories—with familiar Yuletide wares—December sales account for a huge share of the year's sales, over a fifth at jewelry stores, about a sixth at department and discount stores, and about a seventh at clothing, electronics, sporting goods, hobby, and book stores.

What's distinctive about all of this spending is that, except for the prearranged gifts for teenagers, the choices are not made by the ultimate consumers. For the rest of the year, the people who will ultimately use the stuff choose what they buy. As a result, buyers normally choose things they correctly expect to enjoy using. But not at Christmas. As a result, the massive holiday spending has the potential to do a terrible job matching products with users. Throughout the year, we shop meticulously for ourselves, looking at scores of items before choosing those that warrant spending our own money. The process at Christmas, by contrast, has givers shooting in the dark about what you like, recalling the way the imaginary red tornado distributes gifts. To make matters worse, we do much of this spending with credit, going into hock using money we don't yet have to buy things that recipients don't really want.

If you discovered a government program that was hemorrhaging money—say, spending $100 billion of taxpayer money per year to generate a benefit of only $85 billion—you would be outraged. You might even email your elected representatives to demand an end to the wasteful program.

Despite our good intentions, in the private sector we also generate billions less in satisfaction than we could with what we spend. In this book I will show you the size of annual Christmas spending—and the amount that's waste—in the United States and around the world. I'll also show you how present-day Christmas compares to the Christmas of our grandparents, and how we've shifted from saving up for Christmas to maxing out our credit cards to finance the gift storm. I'll make the case that in many circumstances it would be better to not buy presents for the holidays. Finally, I'll point to some solutions that can stop the waste and make holiday giving a force for good.

CHAPTER TWO

Spending and Satisfaction

Advanced decadence is supposed to be a clue
that the End is near. When Romans were holding
orgies in rooms with an en suite vomitorium, you
could guess that Rome would fall. Walk through
a major department store during December. The
aisles are blocked not just with panicked shoppers but also with tables covered with "gift items."
In the aisles near the men's clothing department,
you'll find lots of golf-themed knickknacks—
mugs festooned with golf balls, golf club mittens,
brass tees, and so on. Would anyone buy this stuff
for him- or herself? Does anybody want it? I'll
hazard a "no" on both counts. But it's there every
year, along with singing fish—and it sells—because of a confluence of reasons that together
make a perfect storm for wasteful giving. First,
givers are obliged to get gifts for, say, the distant
relatives they rarely see but will see this year
when they travel to Sacramento for the holidays.
Second, givers want to demonstrate their thought-
fulness by choosing items related to their recipi-

ents' interests. And third, many people, men especially, are known to play golf. (Husband: "Honey, what on earth should I get for your Cousin Ned?" Wife: "He plays golf." Husband: "Got it.") Hence the golf ball candle, or the golf bag wine holder, for Christmas. Cost to society to make: $10. Value to recipient: $0, minus the pain of the forced smile. Some sort of economic apocalypse must be around the corner.

Every year between Thanksgiving and New Year's, newspapers run stories about whether retail spending is on track to beat last year's spending. Is it turning out to be an impressive or a disappointing holiday season? These news articles take the implicit—and often explicit—view that more spending is better. It is true that more spending creates more jobs for workers, more revenue for suppliers, and more profits for retailers. And these are all good things. But is more spending *necessarily* good for society? Forget about our corrupted souls, or our overly materialistic children. I mean, is spending good, even from a narrow economic perspective? The surprising answer is no.

Politicians often cheerlead spending. After the 9/11 attacks on the United States, President Bush encouraged Americans to go about their lives and, in particular, to go shopping. In a September 20 address to the nation, Bush asked

Americans for their "continued participation and confidence in the American economy." The theme emerged again in a 2006 speech: "A recent report on retail sales shows a strong beginning to the holiday shopping season across the country—and I encourage you all to go shopping more."

Spending does create jobs, and jobs are indeed a good thing, in a couple of respects. First, the theoretical. Suppose you would be willing to do your job for as little as $10 per hour. If your pay is $20 per hour, then half your paycheck is essentially a bonus. That's a good thing. At a practical level, jobs provide resources for supporting families, and people without jobs are unhappy and sometimes dangerous.

That said, politicians' focus on job creation in justifying spending reflects a blithe disregard for the taxpayers footing the bill. If our goal were simply to create jobs, we could accomplish that without producing a good or a service of any value. Workers could dig holes, then move them around. Or they could build bridges to remote Alaskan islands.

Spending doesn't justify itself, so how *is* spending normally good for society? A buyer comes into a store and sees a music CD for $15. He buys it only if he expects it to provide a benefit worth more than $15. The difference between the buyer's valuation and the price is a surplus for the buyer, and it's the way that the transaction improves the buyer's life. This surplus is a big deal. When your child is crying all night with an ear infection, you would be willing to pay hundreds or thousands of dollars for a cure. And thanks to modern science, the cure—usually an off-patent antibiotic like amoxicillin—is available for about $20, depending on the co-pay. When you pick up the prescription at the pharmacy, you get a lot of surplus satisfaction out of the transaction.

Assuming we know what we're getting ourselves into, every purchase we make reflects a decision that the value of the item to us—the buyers—exceeds its price. And the difference between our valuation and what we pay is the "consumer surplus" from the transaction.

Walk into a classroom after an economics lecture: both because many economists don't erase and because many lectures feature a demand curve, you'll usually see a diagram with a downward-sloping line. Points along the line represent the most that different people would be willing to pay for a product, ordered from highest to lowest willingness to pay. For example, suppose that Bob is willing to pay $10 for a book, Suzy is willing to pay $9, Ravi is willing to pay $8, and Miguel is willing to pay $7. If the book's price is $7.50, then three of them (Bob, Suzy, and Ravi) buy it. They are each willing to pay more than the price, and their collective willingness to pay ($27) exceeds the amount they collectively pay ($22.50) by the consumer surplus of $4.50. If—as is the case here—the demand curve is a straight line, then consumer surplus is a triangle below the demand curve and above the price. The size of this triangular area represents the amount of consumer surplus, and it's what makes transactions beneficial to consumers. It's the sense in which spending is good, for consumers.

The peculiar thing about consumer surplus is that, unlike the revenue that the sellers get, it does not show up in government statistics. The revenue for amoxicillin does, but most of the parental relief does not. Of course, consumer surplus is related to revenue. When excitement about a product increases—say, we all get interested in iPods—then the demand curve shifts right, and both revenue and surplus increase. But ironically, it's also possible for prices to fall, say because of competition or technological progress, sending the revenue from a product down even as consumer surplus from the product rises. Good examples include penicillin and polio shots. They continue to have enormous benefit, but they are cheap to make. As a result, they generate lots of consumer surplus but little revenue compared with their benefits.

When we make our own consumption choices,

we buy only things that will give us back more satisfaction than we pay, that is, more than the price. For example, when I buy myself a $50 sweater, I buy it only if it's worth at least $50 to me. Gift giving severs the link between the buying decision and the item's value to its user, calling to mind the adage that the road to hell is paved with good intentions. When you buy me a sweater, despite your good intentions and despite how much I like *you*, I may dislike the sweater. At worst, it may be worth nothing to me. Because I did not choose the sweater, there's nothing to guarantee that I will value it above the price you paid. And if I value that sweater below its $50 price—and its $50 cost to society—then rather than creating value, the transaction actually destroys value. For example, if the sweater is worth $25 to me, then giving me the sweater (which cost society $50 to make) reduces society's good fortune by at least $25. You would certainly walk away from an investment opportunity that promised to turn a $50 initial investment into $25. (If not, have I got a deal for you!)

We've all had this experience. From about age ten on—when we first develop well-defined preferences—we endure receiving gifts that we do not like. To make matters even worse, we are obliged to pretend to be grateful.

The cost of getting the wrong thing is actually

a bit worse, as is illustrated by a memorable television commercial for V8 vegetable juice drink. After buying and sipping some other drink—not V8—the actor smacked himself on the head and exclaimed, "I could have had a V8." Head slaps are always funny, so this commercial nicely illustrates the true cost of the choice, what economists term "opportunity cost."

Lemonade and V8 each cost $1. Bill likes V8 so much that, if necessary, he would be willing to pay $2 for a V8 but only $1.50 for lemonade. But—perhaps because of an earlier head injury from smacking himself—Bill sometimes forgets that he prefers V8. What is the cost of his mistaken choice of lemonade? It's $0.50, the difference between the value of the satisfaction he could have bought with V8 and what he did buy with lemonade. Even though Bill gets $1.50 worth of satisfaction from his $1 lemonade, his mistaken choice causes him to miss out on $0.50 in additional satisfaction at the same price. In short, Bill's choice of lemonade destroys $0.50 in value.

Let's return to our government programs to see these ideas in action. These programs create jobs. How can they be bad? They can be bad in the sense that the spending to execute them could have been used to purchase something more valuable to the citizenry. Suppose we need a new school more than we need a new bridge. If each costs $50 million, but the benefit of the school is $75 million while the benefit of the bridge is $25 million, then building the bridge would impose a $50 million loss on society.

Huh? How can that be? We spent $50 million and got back $25 million. The worst possible outcome of this decision would be $25 million in waste, you're thinking. But no. That $50 million expenditure could have produced $75 million in benefit, but instead we got $25 million in benefit. Relative to the $75 million benefit we could have had, we got $50 million less. That's how we wasted $50 million. The true cost of a choice, its "opportunity cost," is one of the very big ideas in economics.

Suppose you have inherited an old house worth a million dollars. It needs a lot of work before you'd want to move in. But you're handy, and you figure you can work on it weekends for the next five years before moving in. Better yet, this won't cost you anything since you inherited the house outright. Wrong! Your local bank will give you something like 5 percent annual interest on deposits. If you sold the house today for $1 million and deposited the proceeds, you'd earn about $50,000 per year in interest. By not doing that— by holding the house for five years—you are sacrificing over a quarter of a million dollars. True, your out-of-pocket cost for holding on to the house without using it is zero. But compared to what you could be earning, the cost is over a quarter of a million dollars. Opportunity cost in action.

The bottom line is that when other people do our shopping, for clothes or music or whatever, it's pretty unlikely that they'll choose as well as we would have chosen for ourselves. We can expect their choices, no matter how well intentioned, to miss the mark. Relative to how much satisfaction their expenditures could have given us, their choices destroy value. Take that, Santa.

A critic might at this point argue that gifts have sentimental value, and including this sentimental value puts the total value of items received as gifts over the top. While I would have been willing to pay only $25 for a $50 sweater I don't much like, its total value to me—including sentimental value—may boost the value of the gift well over the $50 it cost society to make it, say to $75. So, the argument goes, gift giving actually creates, rather than destroys, value. The implausible-sounding key to this defense of unwanted items as gifts is that the sentimental value is conveyed only by items that the recipient does not like. But if the giver had chosen a sweater you actually liked—worth at least $50 to you as a sweater—and if giving that sweater also conveyed the same sentimental value—you'd have something worth at least $100. So, relative to giving you an item you actually wanted, the gift destroyed value.

Is Cash the Paragon, or Could Givers Beat Cash?

We would expect that most gifts, even if thoughtful, are worse than cash. And indeed, according to textbook economic theory applied to gift giving, the best a giver can do, on top of any sentimental value he transmits, is to duplicate the choice—and the satisfaction—the recipient would have purchased for himself with cash.

Under this view, what does efficient giving look like? When your wife buys you a pair of pajamas for Christmas, then if she's astute, first, you actually need a pair of pajamas. It's sensible to defer to her on this one. If she's really astute, then, second, she'll choose the color and style that you would have chosen rather than ones you detest. If both conditions hold, then her gift accomplishes exactly what would be accomplished by a loving suggestion that you should replace your pajamas. That is, it duplicates what you would have done with cash.

Economic theory—and common sense—lead us to expect that buying stuff for ourselves will create more satisfaction, per euro, dollar, or shekel spent, than does buying stuff for others, as I've argued above. Buying gifts typically destroys value and can only, in the unlikely best special case, be as good as giving cash. What a dreary point this book makes, you're thinking by now. If the best a giver can do is to duplicate the effect of cash, then gift giving is about as good an investment as a trip to Vegas, only without Celine Dion and free food. But not necessarily. The notion that people do a good job choosing for themselves is rooted in a rational view of economic decision making that has come under serious attack in recent years.

First, whatever economists like to assume, people are not perfect decision makers. They make bad choices, and it's possible that givers could do better on their behalf. Second, and related, even if people are good at making decisions, they have limited information. Sometimes givers stumble on items they know a recipient would like. Finally, sometimes recipients need permission to enjoy themselves.

These observations recall the lessons of "behavioral economics," an approach to economics that incorporates what psychologists have learned about how people actually make their decisions. People save too little, can't remember what they've liked, can't predict what they'll like, and make other systematic mistakes, such as predicting they'll want more variety than they actually want. So we don't necessarily expect people to do so well making choices.

For a lot of products, even buying for yourself turns out to be hard. A few years ago, for a study of music piracy, I asked a lot of people how high a dollar value they placed on a long list of albums they had purchased. I was not interested in how much they would be willing to pay for the CD at Sam Goody's given that it's also available for $15 down the street at Target. Rather, I wanted to know what the music was really worth to them, so I asked for the maximum they would be willing to pay to get it from a sole hypothetical source. Because CDs typically cost about $15, I had naively expected respondents to report values of $15 and up. To my surprise, the answers were all over the map.

While they reported having paid an average of $15 for the CDs, the average valuation was $13; and about a third of the reported valuations were below the amounts they had reported paying. Part of this was just depreciation. Two years into ownership of a typical Britney Spears album, most people are tired of it and now value it less than they did at purchase. But valuations below prices paid were common even for new albums. Why?

In the old days, before ubiquitous Internet sampling, we used to buy albums based on the one or two songs we'd heard on the radio and our resulting guesses about the quality of the rest. Perhaps not surprisingly, many albums disappointed. Often, the remaining songs were turkeys. To put this in slightly loftier terms, music is an "experience good," or a product whose quality can be evaluated only after it is used. Lots of products are like this: books, movies, drugs, wine, unfamiliar foods, restaurants, medicines. Preferences differ across people, so the fact that others like something is suggestive but not definitive as to whether you'll like it. You don't know whether you'll enjoy it until you try it, so buying any of these products is a hit-or-miss experience. Sometimes they're enjoyable, sometimes not.

This gives an opening for gift givers to outdo our own decision making. Successful buying requires knowledge of our tastes along with knowledge about the item in question. Even granting the shortcomings that psychologists and behavioral economists have identified in our decision making, it's safe to say that we know our own tastes pretty well; and we know a lot about items we've bought before. But we don't know much about items we haven't tried yet. Our givers often know a lot about items unfamiliar to us—they've done some searching—and when our givers know us well, they can be in a position to choose things we might not have picked that will still suit us well.

Cash-Transcending Giving

There are a few kinds of giving that go beyond what the intended recipient would have done for himself. Two kinds of giving that even an economist could admire might be termed "search" and "permission."

I own the original art from the first page of an obscure comic book, *Our Fighting Forces*, number 119, which was issued in June of 1969. I traded a large stack of comic books for it at a comic convention when I was fourteen. For years, intermittently anyway, I rummaged through comic book stores looking for a copy of the issue to display alongside the original art. And for years I was unable to find it.

Suppose you knew I was looking for this issue, and you stumbled on a copy while doing your own shopping, say for *The Amazing Spider-Man* comics. If you picked it up, it would make a terrific gift for me. It would probably have cost you only a few dollars, and I would have been happy to pay $100 for it. If you paid $5 for it, then gave it to me, you would create a surplus of $95 through the purchase, far more than I could typically purchase for myself with $5.

What's going on here? Sometimes it's hard to find the things we want even when we know we want them. The process of looking is termed "search." Economists like to say that there's no free lunch. (I find this puzzling, because many academic economists like me get two or three free lunches a week, at lunchtime seminars and faculty meetings, as well as reimbursed lunches with students.) Still, the "no free lunch" idea is that you can't get something for nothing. The number of things your givers know that you want is far from inexhaustible. Moreover, it is costly for them to search. So this is not a general solution to wasteful gift giving, since it's generally even harder for them to find what you want than it is for you. That is, if you sent them out looking for *Our Fighting Forces*, number 119, they would generally be just as unsuccessful as I had been. But if you know what someone else wants, you can *sometimes* stumble upon something that you can reasonably expect them to appreciate a lot. So giving *can* outdo one's own purchases, particularly for givers who are well informed about their recipients' preferences. But because it's difficult to do this on demand, for all sixty-two of your relatives and acquaintances, Christmas is chal-

lenging. (My story about the elusive comic book—
off the point I'm trying to illustrate—came to a
happy ending when I bought it for a few dollars
on eBay in 2003.)

A second sort of cash-transcending giving, particularly within the family, could be termed "permission." Suppose you know your husband has
been contemplating some indulgent purchase—
an HD TiVo or Blu-ray DVD player. But you've
trained him well, and he's not willing to indulge
himself. His habitual self-abnegation prevents
him from buying this thing that he wants and
would enjoy. What he really needs is permission.
Even if you and he share a bank account, by buy-   20
ing this thing for him, you are granting him permission to get something that he wants. Perhaps   21
in return, you should get permission to buy a hot
tub.

An astute observer will note that both modes
of transcendent giving rely on frictions, or im-
pediments to optimizing behavior, absent in elementary textbook models of the economy. Transcendent search giving arises because information
is costly. If recipients were perfectly informed
about both their preferences and how well they
would enjoy all possible products, then there
would be no way to beat their own choices. Of
course, recipients are not perfectly informed.
The economy produces thousands of new prod-

ucts annually. The music industry alone churns out thirty thousand titles a year. There's no way to be perfectly informed, so of course it's possible that you will know things that your recipients do not know.

Transcendent giving through permission also relies on a friction absent in textbook economic models. The opportunity to make your husband better off by granting permission arises only because he is, well, a blockhead. If he knows—as much as one ever knows—that he really wants a Weber kettle, then he should simply buy it. Maybe he needs to talk it over with his wife, so they can be sure they're making a decision that's sensible for the family. But once they know it's worth more than the price to them and doesn't interfere with their financial planning generally, they should go out and buy it. But people sometimes are blockheads, and when they are, it's possible for gifts to make them better off.

Do not despair completely. Value-creating gift giving is tough, but it's not impossible.

CHAPTER THREE

U.S. Holiday Spending

Theory and common sense suggest that recipients will typically not enjoy their gifts. Yet spend we do! We can measure holiday spending in a variety of ways. The U.S. National Retail Federation (NRF) measures "holiday retail sales" as retail industry sales that occur in the months of November and December. Retail industry sales comprise most traditional retail categories including discounters, department stores, grocery stores, and specialty stores, and exclude sales at automotive dealers, gas stations, and restaurants. In 2007 the NRF forecast holiday sales of $474 billion.

While the NRF approach sensibly excludes expenditures on gasoline—who gives gas as a holiday gift?—it includes all expenditure at the grocery store. And while it may be true that grocery stores get a bump up in sales for the holiday, it's also true that a great deal of spending that occurs during November and December is not gift purchases but rather the usual outlay for groceries and lightbulbs and toilet paper and underwear that goes on all year.

Including all November and December spending, even without gas and automotive purchases, gives rise to an expansive measure of holiday expenditure. What we want is a measure of December spending less the usual maintenance expenditures that happen every month to keep households running. A conservative way to do this is to take the difference between December spending and the spending for an adjacent month that is seasonally similar except that it lacks major gift-giving holidays. This approach gives rise to a restrictive—and conservative—measure of holiday spending, compared with including virtually all retail sales of November and December as holiday spending.

The statistical agencies of most of the major countries provide data on monthly retail sales. These data are available both "raw" and "seasonally adjusted." For most questions—such as "Is the economy growing?"—people rely on the seasonally adjusted data, which remove the systematic month-to-month fluctuations that arise, well, seasonally to reveal the underlying trend. (After monthly fluctuations are eliminated, is the economy growing or shrinking?) But to see the magnitude of holiday spending, we want our sales data the way sushi lovers want their fish, raw. Indeed—as we'll see—holiday spending is the biggest single cause of seasonality in the retail data in most of the developed world.

The U.S. experience in 2007 provides a glimpse into this phenomenon. During 2007 and early 2008, monthly retail spending hovered between $370 and $380 billion most of the year, but in December 2007 spending vaulted to $430 billion, followed by two months of doldrums—January and February—around $345 billion. Although some holiday spending occurs prior to December, notice that November's sales figure, at $381 billion, is only slightly above October's value of $372 billion.

What's different about December in the United States? That's when the major gift-giving holidays fall. How can we use these data to conservatively estimate holiday spending? If all holiday spending fell in December, then December spending less November spending would provide a measure of holiday gift spending. Of course in the United States at least, Thanksgiving (the fourth Thursday in November) is the start of the holiday shopping season, so the retail sales figures for November include some U.S. holiday spending. We see evidence of this in the fact that November retail spending exceeds October's (although not by much). So December spending less November spending—about $49 billion in 2006—

provides a lower-bound estimate of holiday spending.

January provides an alternative to November as a month near December without holiday spending. January spending is typically below November's, so that December spending less the subsequent January's—$83 billion for Christmas 2007—provides a higher estimate of holiday spending in December. Splitting the difference—averaging the December/November and the December/January differences—gives a simple conservative measure of the retail sales for Christmas in 2007, $66 billion. This approach produces an estimate substantially below the NRF estimate, but it's conservative; and the method can be applied to data from around the world (see chapter 5).

Estimates of total holiday spending based on aggregate retail sales statistics can be compared against survey evidence from the variety of annual surveys of holiday gift giving plans. In 2007 Gallup reported a household average of $866, and the Conference Board reported an average of $471. According to the Census Bureau, there are about 110 million households in the United States, so the Gallup and Conference Board spending estimates translate to national holiday spending of $53 billion and $95 billion, respectively, for 2007. These figures are in the ballpark of our estimate of $66 billion, while the NRF estimate implies household holiday spending of $4,300, far above any available household holiday spending estimate derived from surveys.

If it were needed, we could get additional evidence that the December spending spike is gift driven from spending data broken down by category. If the December spike is driven by gift giving, then items typically given as gifts should have disproportionate December spending. Topping the list—for outsized December spending—is jewelry stores, followed by department stores, electronics outlets, and then clothing shops. While December has about 8 percent of the year's shopping days, it has 23 percent of the year's spending at jewelry stores, 16 percent of department stores sales, and 15 percent of sales at electronics stores. These are all common sources for gifts. At the bottom of the list are stores selling items rarely used as gifts: gas stations, garden centers, and car dealers. It is hard to deny that the December retail sales spike in the United States is driven by gift giving for Christmas.

So the first results are in. U.S. holiday spending came to about $66 billion in 2007. All this stuff being purchased by others but, er, enjoyed by you. While not quite literally the economist's nightmare of a red tornado, this nevertheless seems like a recipe for building bridges when we need schools, or drinking lemonade when we really wanted V8. The only way to know is to roll up our sleeves and do some research, then look at the data. I've already done the research, so, in the words of the legendary sports announcer Warner Wolfe, let's go to the videotape!

CHAPTER FOUR

How Much Waste Occurs at Christmas?

Waste, particularly when perpetrated by government, has enemies. For example the nonprofit U.S. group Citizens Against Government Waste, an outgrowth of the Reagan-appointed Grace Commission, scours the annual federal budget looking for programs of dubious value, with benefits below their costs. Their careful review revealed $17.2 billion in waste, which they reported in their annual "pig book" on the 2008 budget. Dubious programs totaling $17.2 billion are a legitimate reason to be mad at Uncle Sam. But the government waste that CAGW identifies pales in comparison with Christmas, so they should save some of their anger for Santa Claus.

The amount of anger Santa deserves depends on how much value giving actually destroys, which, in turn, requires information on satisfaction from items we receive as gifts as well as items we buy for ourselves. How can we determine how satisfying people find their gifts compared to their own purchases? That is, how do we know how much they really like their lemonade relative to the V8 they could have had? I started giving surveys to students when I was an assistant professor at Yale. My students in Econ 150 in the spring of 1993 were willing subjects, probably happier spending ten minutes filling out a survey than listening to ten more minutes of my lecture on—yawn—the intricacies of the demand curve. In early January I asked students to list each of the gifts they had received in the holiday season just finished. For each gift I asked them to indicate the giver's relationship to them (parent, sibling, aunt or uncle, friend, grandparent, or significant other), the amount they thought the giver had paid, and—finally—the dollar value the respondent placed on the item.

The last item turns out to be a bit tricky. It's well known to social scientists that how much people report that something is worth to them depends on how you pose the question. If you ask people how much they are willing to pay for something, they report a low number. If you ask people how much they need to be compensated to give something up, they report a higher number. In my first stab at a survey, I asked people how much they were willing to pay for the gifts they had received, and the average—what I term the "yield"—was only 66 percent of the amounts recipients thought the givers had paid.

If we take the optimistic view that people buy for themselves only things worth at least what they cost, then they would be willing to pay at least what they had actually paid, or 100 percent of the prices of the items. So gift giving would have destroyed at least one-third of the value of the items transferred as gifts.

But given that valuations based on willingness to pay tend to understate, in a second survey, administered in March, I asked students to estimate the value of gifts as the "amount of cash such that you are indifferent between the gifts and the cash, not counting sentimental value of the gift." This time I got an average yield of 87 percent. Again, relative to an assumed 100 percent benchmark for one's own purchases, the fact that these items were chosen by givers rather than ultimate consumers gave rise to at least 13 percent less dollar valuation. Said another way, gift giving destroyed at least 13 percent of the value of the resources transferred.

Economists use the term "deadweight loss" to describe losses to one person that are not offset by gains to someone else. If a dollar disappears from my pocket and reappears in yours, it's a loss to me; but it's not a deadweight loss to society. If you take my dollar and destroy it lighting your Cohiba, then it's a deadweight loss.

At the time of my initial survey, U.S. holiday

spending was roughly $40 billion per year ($62 billion in 2008 dollars). While Yale undergraduates are far richer than the U.S. population as a whole, if the efficiency of their gifts was representative, the range of deadweight loss estimates I had obtained implied $5–$13 billion ($8–$20 billion today) in annual deadweight loss of Christmas. My paper "The Deadweight Loss of Christmas," which appeared in the December 1993 issue of the normally august *American Economic Review*, set off a minor firestorm. The *New York Times* did a story on the paper on December 15. A blushing assistant professor, I appeared on *CBS This Morning* on December 26, on CNN on December 27, and I did scores of radio interviews.

Construing my argument as an attack on Christmas and not just inefficient gift giving, critics—journalists and academics alike—responded. An editorial in the *Chicago Tribune* "suggested that 'flawless gift-giving' has a lesser priority than, say, to 'nurture memories of a great-uncle with a big heart but no taste.'" The editorial concluded that I deserved a loud "Bah, humbug." Academics were concerned—reasonably—that question wording had caused the results.

As I thought about it, I realized the biggest problem with the study was that while people could have had a V8 instead of a lemonade, I had only asked them how much the lemonade was

worth to them. The comparison in the early surveys—to the 100 percent yield benchmark—un-
derstates the inefficiency of gift giving. Just as
you could have had a V8, you could have done
something more satisfying with the money the
giver spent, and maybe you would have gotten
more than a dollar's satisfaction per dollar you
spent. The correct way to calculate the value destruction from gift giving would be to compare
the amount of satisfaction, per dollar spent, derived from items received as gifts with that provided by items people purchased for themselves.
The 100 percent benchmark would be relevant
only if people's purchases for themselves were all
completely borderline, producing satisfaction equal
to the dollar amount spent. Think about a rational consumer: if we buy things for ourselves only
when their valuations meet or exceed the price,
our *average* valuations of our own purchases will
exceed their prices; and the average yield on
items we buy for ourselves will exceed 100 percent. The correct measure of the inefficiency of
allocating via gift giving is, then, the difference
between the yield on gifts and the yield on our
own purchases. Eureka.

Beginning in January 2002, I administered
surveys asking respondents to report value and
price for both items they had received as gifts
and items purchased for themselves. The im-

proved surveys—and I've done four in the United States since 2002—have given consistent results. In addition to being conceptually correct, this approach also gets around the problem that question wording can affect valuation response. I use the same question wording for eliciting valuations of gifts and of individuals' own purchases, and what matters for efficiency is the difference between these two. So even if wording causes over- or understatement of valuations, if it causes the same amount of misstatement for both the gifts and the purchases, then when I subtract one valuation measure from the other, the difference is uncontaminated. And, indeed, people's own choices generate about 18 percent more satisfaction—per dollar spent—than do gifts.

The difference in the averages masks a considerable amount of variation in the yields on both gifts and the purchases people make for themselves. Perhaps surprisingly, just over a third of gifts generate valuations in excess of what recipients think the givers paid. But half of people's own purchases generate higher valuations.

Raw comparisons can be deceiving. That our own purchases generate more satisfaction than do gifts doesn't by itself demonstrate that gift giving destroys value. It's possible that particular items that most recipients dislike—candles?—are used as gifts while people purchase other items—

Batman DVDs—for themselves. For example, if givers are constrained by custom in what they can choose—and if those customs bias giving toward unwanted items—then, to be fair to gift giving, we should compare yields on similar items. If givers gave only music albums and sweaters, then a fair evaluation of gift giving would ask, how much do recipients like the music albums or sweaters that they buy for themselves compared with the music albums or sweaters they receive as gifts. But, no, this does not explain the apparent inefficiency of gift giving. When we make this comparison that "controls for item," we find the same differential, about 19 percent.

34

Perhaps types of recipients differ in how much they like both gifts and their own purchases per dollar spent, but maybe the especially dissatisfied ones get more gifts. Then the difference in the averages would blame giving for the underlying grumpiness of recipients. But, no, this does not explain the result. If we compare yields on gifts and on their own purchases within each recipient, the average difference is 18 percent.

35

I reproduced this survey in January 2007 and January 2008, again with Wharton undergraduates, with nearly identical results. The 18 percent result is robust. Dollars on gifts for you produce 18 percent less satisfaction, per dollar, than dollars you spend on yourself.

We expect people to choose better for themselves because they know their own likes and dislikes better than their givers do. If ignorance of recipient preferences is the reason why givers do poorly, then givers should perform better, the more they know about what the recipient likes.

There's no way of ascertaining directly what givers know about their recipients. But I have consistently asked the giver's relationships to the recipient, whether the giver is a parent, grandparent, sibling, friend, significant other, aunt or uncle. And in a 1994 survey a year after my first surveys, I also asked about frequency of contact between giver and recipient (whether the giver and recipient were in daily, weekly, monthly, or semiannual contact). These two measures are plausibly related to knowledge of recipient preferences. People in frequent contact—and in the same generation—should have more familiarity with their recipients' likes and dislikes. The patterns of yields across groups support giver knowledge of recipient preferences as the key determinant of gift giving efficiency. Distant relatives—who are also substantially older than the college-student gift recipients in the study—fare worst as givers. Aunts and uncles and grandparents generated 80 and 75 cents in recipient satisfaction per dollar spent on noncash gifts. Parents and friends were next, at 97 and 91 cents, respectively. Topping the list were siblings, at 99 cents, and significant others, at 102 cents in satisfaction per dollar spent on their gifts.

Frequency of contact, which could give givers direct information about recipient wants, provides more direct evidence. Putting aside cash gifts, gifts from givers in monthly, weekly, or daily contact generate yields averaging 96 cents per dollar spent, while gifts from givers in only semi-annual contact produced only 86 cents per dollar spent.

Siblings, friends, significant others, and—touchingly—parents do better than others. Who's at risk? Members of the extended family and people in infrequent contact with the recipient. This pattern confirms that poor knowledge of what the recipient wants is responsible for giving that misses the mark.

So there you have it. By my conservative method of reckoning, U.S. givers spent $66 billion in 2007 and produced $12 billion less satisfaction than this expenditure could have bought, for an annual deadweight loss of $12 billion.

If the money expense at Christmas weren't large enough, there is actually another significant cost, the time spent shopping. Since 2003 the U.S. Bureau of Labor Statistics (BLS) has conducted the American Time Use Survey to measure "the amount of time people spend doing various activities, such as paid work, childcare, volunteering, and socializing." From these surveys we know that, of the 24 hours in the day, Americans spent about 9.5 on sleep and grooming, 5 hours on leisure and sports, about 4 hours working (including both workers and others), 1.5 hours eating and drinking, and a little over three-quarters of an hour shopping in 2007. The amount of "time spent purchasing goods and services" varies seasonally in a predictable manner. Except during December, average daily time spent shopping is 55 minutes for women and 38 for men, respectively; in December these jump to 84 and 45 minutes, respectively, for women and men. That's an extra 29 minutes per December day for each woman and an extra 7 minutes for each man. U.S. population is about 300 million and about equally divided by gender. Multiplying additional daily shopping time during the Yuletide season by the number of men and woman—and times the number of days in December—yields 2.8 billion annual hours strolling—and looking for parking—at the mall each Yuletide season, 80 percent of it spent by women. It is not immediately clear how to value this time cost. If it's enjoyable, then it is not really a cost. If it's onerous, then it is a cost and should be added to other elements of cost of Christmas. I'll let you decide for yourself.

The comparison of yields on gifts with the yields on people's own purchases has another use. Behavioral economists have documented many shortcomings in economic decision making that call economists' rationality assumption into question. People don't think enough about the future and therefore do not save enough. They have trouble remembering what they have liked in the past, and trouble predicting what they will want, even in the near future. They underestimate small probabilities of catastrophe and therefore buy too little insurance. Psychologist Daniel Kahneman, who shared the 2002 Nobel Prize in Economics, has argued that "the observed deficiencies [in consumer rationality] suggest the outline of a case in favor of some paternalistic interventions, when it is plausible that the state knows more about an individual's future tastes than the individual knows presently." Similarly, Cass Sunstein and Richard Thaler have advocated a light-handed government intervention in people's lives through what they term "liberal paternalism."

Given all the legitimate concern about shortcomings of decision making, it's worth asking whether people do better at choosing stuff for themselves than others do at choosing for them. The difference between how much people value their gifts and their own purchases, per dollar spent, provides a simple test of whether we are better than others at making simple consumption choices for ourselves. The results indicate that, for all their shortcomings, people do a good job at making simple consumption choices. No one, not the government, not even their close relatives, can outdo their decision making for these simple questions.

If Christmas were a government program, the Citizens Against Government Waste would classify the entire $66 billion in annual expenditure as "waste." CAGW tallies the government programs they deem wasteful: the total expenditure amounted to $17.2 billion in 2008. The actual waste is considerably less, by the amount that citizens benefit from the programs. CAGW members are understandably outraged by $17 billion in spending that produces less than $17 billion in benefit. In Christmas we have $66 billion in the United States that is, on average, wasteful; and we have about $12 billion in actual U.S. value destruction per year. Because of the costs and inefficiencies inherent in a tax system, Arthur Okun famously described government redistribution from rich to poor as a "leaky bucket." The bucket Santa uses—or is it a sleigh?—to bring gifts from givers to recipients isn't just leaking. It's gushing. Can I have some outrage here?

CHAPTER FIVE

*Why We Do It: Are Gift Recipients
Crackheads, or What?*

There are three basic economic reasons to give
people stuff. The first, recalling Robin Hood, is
to take from those who do not need and give to
those, like our poor relations, who do. We call
this "redistribution." The second, recalling the
way parents treat kids and governments treat
crackheads, is to promote sensible consumption
choices. *Wear a hat. Get a prostate exam. Have
some soup, rather than IV drugs*. We call this second motive "paternalism." The third motive, to
make recipients as satisfied as possible, is the way
we treat loved ones whom we trust to make good
choices. This is called "altruism."

To think about the goal of Christmas givers,
it's useful to juxtapose private Christmas giving
with government's various forms of giving, including in-kind grants of food stamps, housing
vouchers, and—sometimes—cheese. Beyond this,
we need a way of thinking about when cheese is
cheese and when cheese is effectively cash. The
questions we need to answer are these: (1) What

would recipients do with cash? (2) Do we want to alter their consumption relative to what they would do with cash?

While Christmas giving—as we've seen—is huge, private giving is actually small potatoes compared with the amount of resources—money, food and housing vouchers, medical care reimbursement—given directly to citizens by the U.S. government. A lot of government largesse is given in restricted fashion, either as vouchers for particular things or, literally, "in kind," meaning given as cheese rather than cash. The U.S. food stamp program gives out $30 billion per year in food vouchers. Public housing expenditures—free or discounted housing or vouchers for housing—total about $25 billion per year. Primary and secondary education—half a trillion per year—is largely given out free by local governments. Even market reformers advocate vouchers, which are essentially gift certificates redeemable only at educational institutions. The list goes on. School lunch programs give lunches to kids of low-income families. The largest government gift is medical care reimbursement, both for poor people (through Medicaid) and for the elderly (Medicare). The total annual government "gift" budget in the United States easily dwarfs Christmas giving.

In-kind transfers are a puzzle if you think that

transfer recipients are well suited to make their own consumption choices. We've already encountered one of the first lessons in college economics, the inferiority of in-kind transfers to cash grants. Why is this so? People have their own preferences, and these preferences are hard for the government to know. (As we've seen, they're hard for your parents to know, so Uncle Sam is at an even larger disadvantage.) If the goal of the transfers is to promote the most possible satisfaction for the recipients, we should give them cash and let them decide what to buy. Don't give them $10 worth of cheese; give them $10. The proof of the superiority of cash is as simple as this: One of the things recipients can do with the $10 is buy $10 worth of cheese. If that's what they would have done, then—bingo—the government program is perfectly efficient. But if the recipients would have done something else, then the government program is not efficient. That is, by giving cheese rather than money, the program prevents them from being as happy as possible with an expenditure of $10.

But cheese is sometimes cash. How can this be? Imagine that you are planning your monthly spending. You budget money for all of the things you'll buy this month. Let's say your plan includes $15 for cheese. Now imagine redoing your budgeting knowing that the government is giving you

$10 worth of cheese. You can now reduce your own cheese expenditures to $5, which frees up $10 that you can use for cheese or anything else. In effect, the big hunk of cheese is a $10 cash grant from the government. Good news for the recipient, but potentially bad news for the giver.

If the giver's goal is to change behavior, it's not enough to give the healthy thing—bran, let's say—that you want them to eat. You also must give more bran than the recipient currently eats, that is, when he's getting by without a grant. Any amount of bran he's already eating—up to the amount of the grant—becomes cash, since he can substitute the gift bran for purchased bran, freeing up cash for anything else he might buy.

Government Giving

Given all this, what are we trying to accomplish with government gifts? Most grants-in-kind are actually vouchers, as with housing and food, with the flexibility to allow them to function more like cash. But—and this is important—food stamps are cash only if the amount of food stamp–eligible food you were planning to buy absent food stamps exceeds the value of the stamps. If with your meager pre–food stamp budget you could afford only $20 worth of healthy staples per month and the program gives you $50 usable to-

ward healthy staples, then the stamps increase
your healthy staple consumption from $20 to at
least $50. If, with the grant, you consume healthy
staples worth $70, there's no cash left over; if you
consume an amount worth, say, $60, then the
stamps free up $10 in cash.

From the trusted free consumer's standpoint,
the possibility of cheese being cash is great news:
despite the clumsiness of government giving, the
cheese recipients were able to turn the gift into
cash and do with it whatever they wanted. As a
concerned taxpaying citizen, you may be scratch-
ing your head. Wait a minute—I thought we gave
out cheese to ward off starvation. If cheese is
cash, then cheese is—substitute your worst mar-
ketable vice here—crack, crystal meth, Bud Lite.
As a taxpayer, you may want to see that those
given cheese actually consume more cheese than
they would have without the government gift.

And indeed, the designers of the food stamp
program were not attempting to simply enable
more overall consumption. They were seeking to
raise the caloric intake of kids in poor families
(think of a simpler time before the poor in the
United States were disproportionately obese). The
food stamp and school lunch programs are supposed to prevent hunger among poor kids. And
the public and subsidized housing programs are
supposed to give poor families adequate places to

44

45

live, to prevent their having to double up with other families in unhealthy tenements.

The reason we make government grants in kind is that we do not trust the recipients to choose wisely. We are worried that if we gave them cash, then rather than feed or house their kids, poor people might buy liquor (or worse). So many observers deem these programs a success the *less* they are like cash. These programs are paternalistic and not altruistic. Policy makers and taxpayers alike want to dictate the amounts spent on food, housing, medical care, and education. In particular, we want to ensure that kids get more than some bare minimum. And while some of the cheese turns to cash, the programs are targeted at people sufficiently poor that even cheesy cash is mostly spent on necessities of the sort that the programs seek to promote. Government giving is paternalistic.

What about the pattern of giving and receipt across households? Government "gifts" in cash and in kind are financed with general tax revenue and given to low-income households. The government's giving also recalls Robin Hood: it redistributes from richer to poorer at the same time that it is paternalistic.

So the lessons from Uncle Sam's giving are two. First, we seek to change behavior in ways that we deem healthy. But second, this is hard, given that "gifts" can free up cash that can be used to buy anything.

Private Giving

At first blush the lessons of Uncle Sam's giving are not relevant to private Christmas giving. Our gift recipients are not, for the most part, crack addicts. We do trust their preferences. But the more we trust their own preferences, the more inclined we are—implicitly—to try to ape what they would have done with cash. You can't tell anything to the man who knows everything. Similarly, if whatever you buy your recipient is either what he would have purchased—unlikely—or something he has considered and rejected, then you're playing a sucker's game.

All of this raises the question of what givers are trying to accomplish with their holiday gifts. Are they trying to altruistically promote as much satisfaction as possible for their recipients? Or are they trying to steer their recipients paternalistically toward healthy consumption choices?

Cash and the Motivation for Giving

As we have seen earlier, economic theory tells us that altruism would be best implemented through straight cash giving. Yet holiday cash giving is too rare to indicate that altruism is the major motive for Christmas gifts. So the motivation must be something besides altruism, perhaps paternalism . . .

Not so fast.

"Cash" is not the first word that comes to mind for most people when they hear "Christmas gift." But cash is a relatively common gift to college students. About one in seven gifts in the samples from my 1993 and 1994 studies were cash or gift certificates. Eight percent of the gifts in the 2002 sample were cash or gift certificates (half of each). The low overall tendency to give cash obscures highly elevated cash giving from extended family members and virtually nonexistent cash gifts from friends, boyfriends, and girlfriends. In the 1993 sample, a third of gifts from aunts and uncles were cash or gift certificates, as were over half of the gifts from grandparents. Only 1 percent of the gifts from significant others were either cash or even gift certificates.

What can we learn from these decisions to give cash? To answer this, we have to think about the nature of cash as a gift. First off, at least in some circumstances, cash is a tacky gift. A large body of research in psychology documents that in many circumstances, cash is a socially awkward gift. Cash is particularly inappropriate as a gift from younger to older people. Cash is considered socially acceptable from parents or grandparents to children, but it's unacceptable from kids to parents. It's hard to imagine giving cash to your girlfriend. Unless, of course, she's a "working girl," and she's not really your friend. But that's a different topic. It's similarly difficult to imagine giving cash to your friend or siblings at Christmas. On the other hand, cash gifts from parents and grandparents seem quite natural and common.

Given the social constraints on cash giving, the rarity of cash gifts does not, by itself, rule out altruism as the givers' motive. If givers don't like to give cash because it's awkward, then one interpretation is that there is effectively a "cash stigma" that functions like a tax. If you give them $100 in cash, you get only as much benefit as if you gave them, say, $80 without any awkwardness. That is, they get the full $100, but the ickiness of getting it in cash makes them feel only as happy as they would feel stumbling on four $20 bills.

Under the stigma view, cash is a handicapped gift in that it certainly results in less value for the recipient than what I spend. While it has a low return, however, it also has low risk. If I don't know what you like and I buy you a noncash gift, I run the risk of destroying the full value of what I spend. If you hate country music, and I buy you a $100 Waylon Jennings box set, I can easily turn the $100 into $0 worth of satisfaction. Unless the implicit cash tax is 100 percent, the cash gift safely transfers the after-tax value of the cash gift amount and beats Waylon.

Given all this, we should be able to learn something about giver motives from the pattern of cash giving. First off, given that gifts usually destroy value, the rarity of cash gifts is prima facie evidence of a cash stigma if givers are altruistic. If cash carried no stigma, then—except when givers had strong reason to believe they had found something recipients value highly but would not purchase for themselves—gifts would all be cash. Most gifts are not cash, so there must be some stigma associated with giving it. And since there is a cash stigma, each giver has to decide, based on his gift-giving acumen, whether to give cash or a conventional gift.

What would altruism look like in conjunction with a stigma of cash giving? Depending on the size of the stigma, cash gifts could be either common or rare. But cash gifts would be more common from givers with the most trouble choosing appreciated noncash gifts. This is what we see. The givers whose noncash gifts are least appreciated, per dollar spent—aunts and uncles and grandparents—are also the most likely to give cash. Similarly, givers in less frequent contact with recipients are more likely to give cash. The variation across ethnic groups is also consistent with the altruistic goal of promoting recipient satisfaction. Jews and Asians have the lowest yield on noncash gifts and the highest tendency to get cash gifts. It's not possible to distinguish between inept givers and ungrateful recipients as the joint determinants of low yields and elevated cash giving. But in either case the pattern is consistent with cash chosen to avoid anticipated value destruction. In a word, the pattern is consistent with altruism.

For example, grandparents, who typically see their grandchildren only a few times per year, know little about what the grandkids want for Christmas. As any grandparent knows, choosing a conventional gift is a gamble with unfavorable odds. On average, noncash gifts from grandparents produce yields of 75 percent. Not surprisingly, more than half of the gifts from grandparents in the 1993 sample were cash. Friends, who tend to see each other frequently, know a lot about each other's possessions and desires. Their noncash gifts produce yields of 91 percent, and only 2 percent of their gifts are cash.

The negative relationship between cash giving and the yield on noncash gifts, which would arise if givers were altruistically trying to avoid wasteful giving, survives more rigorous analysis. We

50

51

can divide the 2,400 gifts in the 1993 sample into groups based on relationship between giver and recipient (6 groups: parents, friends, grandparents, aunts/uncles, significant others, siblings), frequency of contact between giver and recipient (4 groups: daily, weekly, monthly, a few times per year), and recipient religion/ethnicity (3 groups: Protestant non-Asians, Catholic non-Asians, and Jews combined with Asians). Of the resulting 72 subgroups, 46 have enough gifts in each cell for meaningful analysis. For each cell we can compute two numbers, the average yield on noncash gifts and the share of gifts that are cash. If people in the group have an idea of their gift-giving acumen, and if the goal of giving is to produce satisfaction for recipients, then the cells with lower average yields on noncash gifts should have high tendencies to give cash. This is exactly what we find, and it's consistent with altruism in conjunction with a cash stigma.

The pattern of cash giving across gifts of different prices is separately interesting and reveals something about the structure of the stigma. Very few gifts under $25 are cash, while the share of gifts that are cash rises steadily with the value of the gift—cash or stuff—given. This pattern suggests that the stigma of cash is not simply proportional to the amount spent. If the stigma of cash giving were a constant 20 percent, then the tendency to choose cash would not depend on the size of the gift. A $100 cash gift would produce $80 worth of satisfaction, while a $10 gift would produce $8. If I were a reasonably good giver—say, I could achieve 90 percent yield—then I would choose a noncash gift in either case. If I spent $100, I would expect to produce $90 worth of satisfaction with a gift of $100, while I would expect to produce $9 with a gift of $10. For a gift of either size, I would beat cash with a noncash gift. If I expected to produce a 70 percent yield, I would give cash for either size gift. But for either type of giver, the cash tendency would be independent of the size of the gift.

The rarity of small cash gifts indicates that whatever satisfaction cash destroys looms larger for gifts of smaller absolute size. A natural explanation for this is a stigma of cash giving that includes both a fixed component and a variable component.

Suppose that when you give a cash gift, the value the recipient attaches to it is $10 less, regardless of how much you give. Then if you had $10 for a gift, you would never give it as cash, since the recipient would value it at $0. You also would not generally give $20 bills as gifts, since you could probably beat a 50 percent yield with a noncash gift. If you had $100 to give, though, your decision might change. Now you can beat cash only if you can choose a noncash gift—a sweater or bowling ball, say—that produces a yield above 90 percent. Not impossible but harder than beating the 50 percent threshold on a $20 gift. This mechanism—a cash stigma that includes a fixed component—can explain the pattern we see in the data: a cash-giving tendency that rises in the amount given.

If the stigma included only a fixed component, then cash would become dominant for large gifts, as the threshold that noncash gifts would need to beat approached 100 percent. Yet, in the data, even for gifts of over $100, only 20 percent are cash. This means that the stigma includes both a fixed and a proportional component.

Indeed, if we take the data quite literally, we can infer the structure of the stigma from the pattern of cash giving. Overall, the best estimate of the stigma is a flat fee of $4 plus about half the amount of cash given. So if you give $100, the awkwardness of cash makes the gift worth less to the recipient. It's like getting about $45 with no tacky strings attached. This stigma is large, and it explains the rarity of cash gifts.

What about redistribution? Recall that "gifts" from the government are targeted disproportionately at low-income households. U.S. data on income by source show a different pattern. While the value of gifts makes up a larger share of the income of the poorest households—the value of gifts received is about 4 percent of household income for households with incomes under $20,000—for higher-income households the share is steady at 2 percent. Rather than redistributing from rich to poor, for the most part private gifts reinforce the advantage of the rich.

Private gift giving, unlike government transfers, seeks to promote recipient satisfaction, rather than to constrain recipient consumption choices. The only reason that so much Christmas giving is in-kind rather than cash is the stigma of cash giving. If we take a hyperliteral view of giving, the stigma of cash giving is the sole reason for the inefficiency of Christmas giving. If there were no stigma, then givers would give cash, and recipients would choose items that they really want, resulting in the most possible satisfaction given the amounts spent.

54

55

Identifying a dysfunctional institution and improving it are two different things. Tell an American, "Darn it, you have ten fingers, so you could keep track of size, temperature, and mass more easily using the metric system." You will get an incredulous stare, and you'll be run out of town. The metric system is unnatural to us, or, to put it another way, it creates very little—and very possibly negative—satisfaction. "Ignore your distaste for giving cash, and give cash gifts" is about as effective as "use the metric system" in changing behavior. The cash gifts we currently see are Grandma's cry for help: "Please let me be more efficient." While gift certificates are making some important inroads—more on that in a subsequent chapter—for the foreseeable future we seem to be stuck with a need to give, in conjunction with strong cultural restrictions on giving cash. Santa has stuck us between a rock and a hard place, and as a result, American Decembers will bring dead-weight losses for as far as the mind's eye can see.

CHAPTER SIX

Giving and Waste around the World

Americans have a worldwide reputation for excess. We make up only 5 percent of world population, yet we consume a quarter of the world's gasoline, complaining bitterly about gas prices even as we pay about half what Europeans pay. We're well known for excess in other areas. We drive big cars. We live in large houses on large plots of land sprawled far from city centers (hence the need for all those cars). Finally, we're fat. According to the World Health Organization, 32 percent of American men, and 38 percent of women, were obese in 2002. The only countries ahead of us on the 194-country male obesity list were western Pacific island nations such as Tonga and Samoa. We lag behind in female obesity. Stouter women waddle across not only western Pacific nations but also Kuwait, Jordan, Egypt, the UAE, Barbados, Trinidad, and Dominica. A nation of voracious appetites, surely we also lead the pack in vulgar excess at Christmas. Or maybe not.

We've seen how much Americans spend on holiday gifts each year—$60 to $90 billion based on the difference between December and, respectively, November and January monthly retail sales. What about the rest of the world? What about the culturally sophisticated Europeans, the hardworking and productive Asians, the up-and-coming Latin Americans, or the poor Africans? Do they, like us, celebrate Christmas as a commercial extravaganza? And if they do, is their gift giving inefficient like ours?

In order to answer these questions, we need the worldwide counterparts to the nonseasonally adjusted monthly retail sales data that illustrated the U.S. holiday spending. Fortunately, the Organization of Economic Co-operation and Development (OECD) collects data on its member countries (European countries, plus the United States, Canada, Australia, Japan, Korea, and Turkey), as well as other countries it has either invited to join (such as Russia and Israel) and still others with which the OECD has "enhanced engagement" (such as China, Brazil, and South Africa). Among all these, the OECD has monthly retail sales data on thirty-two countries.

The OECD has monthly retail sales for some countries going back to the 1960s. The OECD data do not generally report the actual value of sales in a given month; instead, they typically report indices that show the proportionate change from one month to the next. These data are still useful for determining the Yuletide spending bump, the percent by which December retail sales exceed those in adjacent months or the share of total retail sales attributable to Christmas spending.

Using the data from the OECD, we are able to compare the U.S. December sales bump to thirty-one other countries. The data cover the main predominantly Christian economic powers of North America and Western Europe, along with three major Asian economies (Korea, Japan, China), Eastern European countries such as Russia emerging from communist suppression of religious practice, and the world's only predominantly Jewish country, Israel.

The countries differ not only in religious composition but also in income, running the gamut from northern Europe and the United States, with over $40,000 in per capita GDP, to countries like Israel, Portugal, and Korea, with about $20,000 in per capita GDP, all the way to countries like Poland, Mexico, Russia, Brazil, and South Africa (all averaging between $5,000 and $10,000) and China with just over $2,000 in per capita annual GDP (all in 2006 U.S. dollars).

Do other countries besides the United States have a Christmas spending bump? And if they do, is it confined to the predominantly Christian nations? Does it appear in rich nations, poor nations, or both? Is the practice of allocating resources through holiday gift giving a luxury that arises only in countries rich enough to afford substantial value destruction? Or does it happen in poor countries as well? And finally, what has happened to Christmas spending over the years?

Let's start our comparison with Western Europe, a region whose countries are culturally and economically similar to the United States. That is, they are predominantly Christian; and they are rich. Their populations resemble Americans in another respect: most Americans have European ancestors. When we examine monthly retail sales data from January 2007 to February 2008 for fourteen Western European countries, we see that each country has an unmistakable December sales spike, much as the United States does.

How about Eastern Europe? These countries have substantially lower per capita income, but except for Russia, where 59 percent report being Christian, Eastern Europe is as predominantly Christian as the West. And, indeed, the five Eastern European countries represented in the data—the Czech Republic, Hungary, Russia, Poland, and the Slovak Republic—also had unmistakable December sales spikes in 2007.

Given its century of godless communism, Rus-

sia's Yuletide spike is surprising. In 1917 Bolshe-
viks banned Christmas in Russia, replacing the
Star of Bethlehem with the red five-pointed Soviet star. The fir tree was also banned as a Christmas symbol, although the tree returned to Soviet Russia in 1933 as "the New Year Tree." On
Stalin's order in 1933, "the Cathedral of Christ
the Saviour was dynamited and reduced to rub-
ble." During communist rule, Russians celebrated
Christmas only privately and "at risk of losing
their jobs, freedom and even lives." We continue
our comparison with lower-income countries,
such as Brazil, Mexico, and South Africa. These
countries, too, had large December sales spikes   60
in 2007. Mexico and Brazil are predominantly
Catholic. South Africa is 82 percent Christian.   61

Among the countries we study, the only ones
without a December sales spike in 2007 were Israel, China, and South Korea, where Christians
are rare. And these patterns appear not only in
2007 but in every year the data cover, back to the
1960s.

Of the countries with the smallest December
retail bumps, most are Asian. However, Japan
has a small but noticeable December bump, and
this is curious in that less than 1 percent of its
population is Christian. That Japan gets a 21 percent bump is surprising given its almost complete
innocence of Judeo-Christian traditions. In re-

cent years Japanese have treated Christmas as a commercial event with gift giving and a traditional "Christmas cake" and the *daiku*, or Great Nine, a performance of Beethoven's Ninth Symphony.

If the December spike in retail activity in most of the world is driven by Christmas, then one place we should not see it is Israel. Although American Jews exchange gifts at the Jewish holiday of Hanukah, which typically falls in December, Israelis do not. And indeed, there is no December spike in Israel's retail sales index.

Israel's retail pattern does include some seasonal spikes, in spring and fall. The reason is that the major gift giving holidays in Israel are Passover, which generally occurs in April, and the Jewish New Year, Rosh Hashanah, which occurs in September or October. (Jewish holiday timing is dictated by a lunar calendar, so the Jewish holidays can move across months.)

So there is a December Yuletide sales spike— a percentage excess of December sales over the two adjacent months—in most developed countries. But how do the countries compare? And where is the United States on the list? To examine this, we compute the Yuletide bump for each country, then average this across years since 2000.

The largest December bumps—35 to 50 percent above adjacent months—occur in Hungary,

Italy, Portugal, Brazil, Norway, and South Africa. The smallest—under 10 percent—occur in Korea, Israel, China, and Ireland. The United States— at just under 25 percent—is at the lower end of the middle of the pack, between Spain and Germany. The United States ranks twenty-first among thirty-one countries with the requisite data for calculating Yuletide bumps since 2000.

December retail sales spikes calculated for each decade back to the 1960s reveal similar patterns, with many of the same countries occupying top- and bottom-ranked locations. Coverage varies across years, but the United States is never even above the median country.

Christmas has a large effect on the economy in some surprising places. Christmas returned officially to Russia in 1991 when it was established as a Russian Federation holiday. By Christmas 1996 the *New York Times* described Russian Christmas as an "adoration of the monetary," reporting that Russians had "borrowed many Western holiday traditions." While Russians had traditionally celebrated Christmas in early January, in 1996 merchants began putting up "Christmas decorations and promotional displays in October."

Russian retail statistics are available back to 1994 from the OECD. A comparison of the December retail bump in Russia and the United States confirms that the Russian retail bump has

62

63

not only grown quickly since 1994; it also over-took the U.S. retail bump in 2005. That's right: Russia's proportional excess of December retail sales over adjacent months now exceeds that of the United States. Kubrick's fictional General Buck Turgidson, played memorably by George C. Scott in *Dr. Strangelove*, worried about a post-nuclear U.S. "cave gap" behind the Russians. Thankfully, nuclear war and concerns about cave gaps did not come to pass. But what would Buck have thought about the emerging Santa Claus gap?

Perhaps not surprisingly, the larger December retail sales bumps appear in countries with pro-portionately larger Christian populations. The positive relationship is largely due to the compar-ison between non-Christian countries (Israel and Asian nations) and the predominantly Christian countries of the rest of the sample. But even with the non-Christian countries removed, a faint pos-itive relationship remains.

The December spikes around the predomi-nantly Christian parts of the world confirm that Christmas has a noticeable effect in many econo-mies. But the spike shows how much December spending towers over adjacent months, and does not directly indicate how much Christmas spend-ing occurs in each country. To calculate the value of Christmas spending—not just its value relative to other months—we need to know the volume of annual retail sales in total for each country. These data are hard to come by, but consultancy Euromonitor Incorporated provides consistent data on annual retail sales for many countries of the world, including twenty-six that overlap with countries in our study.

The OECD retail sales indices allow us to calculate the share of a year's retail sales attributable to Christmas. Multiplying this by the Euromonitor annual retail sales data gives total Christmas sales by country. Finally, dividing this by population gives something easily comparable across countries, per capita Christmas sales. This is a direct measure of spending, with no adjustment for countries' income levels. Not surprisingly, rich countries dominate the top of the list, and poor countries dominate the bottom. But there are actually two ways to show up at the bottom of the list: being poor and lacking interest in Christmas. The bottom six countries, reflecting one or both of these reasons, are, in descending order: Mexico (with $46 in per capita Christmas sales per year, in 2006 dollars), South Africa ($31), Brazil ($24), Israel ($13), Korea ($9), and China ($4). The top end is dominated by countries that are both rich and enthusiastic about Christmas. The top five, in descending order, are Norway ($288), the United Kingdom ($215), Italy ($212), Finland ($211), and France ($191). The United States is twelfth among the twenty-six countries, nestled between Belgium and Portugal, with $140 in annual per capita Christmas spending. (Note that because the Euromonitor national retail sales numbers deviate from the U.S. retail sales numbers, the implied U.S. spending differs from that calculated with U.S. retail sales data.)

In some ways spending as a share of income provides a more accurate measure of the emphasis that a country's people place on Christmas. We can divide Christmas spending by gross domestic product to produce an index of Christmas spending per million dollars of GDP. This normalization reorders the countries considerably. Countries with relatively few Christians—China, Israel, and Korea—still dominate the bottom of the ranking. But moderate-income Christian countries—such as Mexico, South Africa, and Brazil—shoot up to the top. In descending order the top countries in Christmas sales relative to GDP are Portugal ($7 per million in GDP), Italy (6.5), South Africa (5.8), Mexico (5.7), and the United Kingdom (5.4). The United States is twentieth on this list of twenty-six countries, with just over $3 in spending per million in GDP, between Japan and Germany.

American Christmas may be overly commercial and materialistic. But we are not alone. Unlike our ranking on obesity or gasoline consumption—where we beat all major comers—our ranking on holiday spending is more typical, perhaps even below average, for a country of our wealth and religious makeup. To say this another way, the phenomenon of massive holiday spending prevails throughout Christendom.

Is Spending Wasteful throughout Christendom?

It's clear that a lot of resources get allocated through holiday gift giving throughout the world. Is there any reason to think gift giving is as wasteful elsewhere as well? To get some insight into this, I had my survey administered at sites in Sweden, Germany, Belgium, Spain, England, and Brazil in January 2008. The samples were unfortunately not all large, but I was able to ask the question in a variety of places.

As in the recent U.S. surveys, I asked respondents both about items they had received as gifts and items they had recently purchased for themselves. Among the 1,053 items that were neither cash nor gift certificates in the European samples, those received as gifts were 9 percent less valuable to the recipients than were items those people bought for themselves, per dollar spent on them. For South America, the loss was 47 percent.

The international results mirror many aspects of the American results. Gifts from siblings, friends, and significant others generate about as much satisfaction as people's own purchases. On the other hand, gifts from aunts and uncles and grandparents generate significantly less. The 2008 international surveys contained one category that did not appear in previous surveys, in-laws, as possible givers. In their first scientific outing, in-laws turned out to be the least able givers: their gifts generated over a third less value per dollar spent than did their recipients' own purchases.

We get a little more evidence on the universality of bad gifts from India. While India has very few Christians and therefore little Christmas celebration to speak of, its major gift-giving holiday is Diwali, which, recalling the Jewish Hanukah, is called the Festival of Light. Falling in October or November, depending on the lunar calendar, Diwali is a major occasion of gift giving. An exact text search of "Diwali gift" on Google (on July 31, 2008) generated "about 45,000" pages. ("Christmas gift" generated just over 9 million the same day).

In February 2006 two scholars at the Kohinoor Business School in Khandala, India, conducted a survey to measure the deadweight loss of Diwali gifts among a sample of students in India. They note that the practice of giving Diwali gifts beyond the immediate family has grown over the past decade as India's income has grown. Using a sample of seventy-four students, they asked only about items received as gifts, and they found an average gift yield of 85 percent, very similar to the results found in the United States. Other findings also mirror those from the U.S. and European data. Gifts from siblings, cousins, and friends have the highest yields. Yields on gifts from aunts and uncles and grandparents are lowest.

So the world data are in, and there's good news and bad news. First, the good news. America is not the undisputed world leader in materialistic holiday festivities. Our gift giving is no more excessive than, say, that of France. *Touché*! If we're grading on an international curve, the U.S. Yuletide grade is OK even if we're failing elementary gas consumption and still need to hit the gym.

But the bad news probably outweighs the good. In 2007 the deadweight loss of Christmas for the United States alone, with roughly $66 billion in retail sales for the holiday, was about $12 billion. We now see that the phenomenon is not restricted to the United States. Including the twenty-six countries with both OECD retail sales indices and Euromonitor sales data, total world retail sales for Christmas gifts in 2006 topped $145 billion, and there's reason to believe that the deadweight losses that have been repeatedly documented in the United States appear in other countries. So the worldwide waste during 2006 topped $25 billion. Ouch. Is anyone even concerned about this? Santa is a beloved figure, but this is ridiculous.

CHAPTER SEVEN

A Century of American Yuletide Spending

We tend to think that American grownups of the early and mid-twentieth century were serious, hardworking people who built the country into a world power. The twentieth century of popular imagination was peopled by the "greatest generation," men who—literally—soldiered on and saved the world without grousing about their feelings. And for much of the twentieth century U.S. women devoted their labors to the domestic front. With the combination of serious men and hardworking women at home baking cookies for the holidays, Christmas surely could not have been the commercial extravaganza we have made it.

Or was it?

Just as every generation imagines that it invented sex, every generation imagines that it invented the vulgar commercialization of Christmas. A detailed look at a century of U.S. spending patterns demonstrates—perhaps surprisingly—that contemporary holiday spending is neither unique nor excessive compared to that of the past century.

The U.S. government has kept excellent records of monthly retail sales for nearly a hundred years. Since 1935 monthly retail sales data have been available both overall and in specific categories within durable and nondurable goods. The available narrow categories below durables include building materials, furniture and appliances, and automobiles, as well as jewelry. Nondurable categories include stores selling apparel, shoes, food, and general merchandise (department stores). The nondurable categories also include restaurants and sales of gasoline, drugs, and liquor. Clearly, these categories span a spectrum from those highly relevant to holiday giving, such as jewelry and general merchandise stores, to the irrelevant, such as gas stations and car dealerships. Prior to 1935, and beginning in 1919, the U.S. government reported monthly indices of retail sales at mail-order houses, ten-cent stores, and chain stores in various categories such as groceries, clothing, drugs, cigars, shoes, and candy.

In the first chapter we documented a December retail sales bump. Is that a recent phenomenon, or has it happened before? A graph of monthly nonseasonally adjusted retail sales throughout the 1990s looks like an EKG for an increasingly irritated cartoon character. The increasing irritation is the trend growth in the value of retail sales, due to both price growth and real increase in the amount of stuff sold. The "heartbeats" are, of course, the jumps in retail sales that each December brings. The same pattern appears in the 1980s, the 1970s, and earlier.

We can examine the December bump, relative to adjacent months, back to 1935. To do this we calculate two indices: the percent by which each December exceeds the immediately preceding month (November), and the percent by which December exceeds the immediately following month (January). Except perhaps during the Great Depression, when it was a bit lower than afterward, it is stable. December exceeds the immediately following January by an average of 34 percent, and December's retail sales exceed November by an average of 19 percent. There are annual fluctuations. Recession years such as 1974 are low, and boom years such as 1985 are high. But there is no trend overall. The bottom line is that the Yuletide bump has not grown since the mid-1930s.

How about before 1935? Prior to 1935 retail sales statistics were reported in different ways. Instead of reporting total retail sales along with sales by exhaustive categories that together made up the total, the U.S. government collected data for particular large retailers. This brings us to the retail landscape of the turn of the last century.

The mail-order houses were the retail juggernauts of the day. Sears was the largest, with $3.1 billion (in year 2007 dollars) sales in 1919. Montgomery Ward was second, with 1919 sales of $1.3 billion in year 2007 dollars. (For comparison, Wal-Mart sales in 2007 were $388 billion.) The largest of the ten-cent ("dime") stores was Woolworth's with 1919 sales of $1.2 billion (again in 2007 dollars). Combined, the four top mail-order houses, along with the top four ten-cent stores and the largest department store (Penney's) had sales equaling nearly a percent of national income. By contrast, Wal-Mart revenue today is nearly 3 percent of GDP. While not nearly as dominant as Wal-Mart today, these enterprises were large. And more important, their sales patterns provide a good snapshot of retail sales patterns of the day.

So was there a December bump prior to 1935? The earliest year with systematic data is 1919, when the government statistics reported monthly data for mail-order houses, as well as grocery chains, ten-cent stores, and chains in apparel, drugs, cigars, shoes, and candy. Most of these categories exhibit pronounced seasonal patterns, although groceries do not, because groceries are useful all year round and not particularly useful as gifts. All plunge after December. Most of the rest—including apparel, drugs, shoes, and especially ten-cent and candy stores—jump from November to December.

Mail-order houses are slightly different but still heavily affected by Christmas. Their sales jump in October and remain high through the end of the year, although December sales are lower than November sales. These are catalog sales, largely from Sears and Montgomery Ward. Although they were probably not delivered on a Wells Fargo wagon in 1919, the lyrics of the "Wells Fargo Wagon" song from *The Music Man* are nevertheless instructive: "O-ho the Wells Fargo Wagon is a-comin' down the street, Oh please let it be for me!" The song continues, "Montgom'ry Ward sent me a bathtub and a cross-cut saw." That bathtub probably had to be ordered in October for December delivery across the Rocky Mountains.

The December bumps at apparel, drug, cigar, and shoe stores were moderate to large, averaging 21 percent relative to November and 55 relative to January. But the bumps at dime and candy stores were enormous. Relative to adjacent months, December 1919 saw 98 and 70 percent increases in sales at dime and candy stores, respectively. Given the importance of dime stores such as Woolworth's, it's convenient that we are able to document the December dime-store bump for eight years following 1919. The year 1919 was no exception. The December bump at dime stores appeared throughout the 1920s. Relative to January, the bump actually grew fairly steadily from 120 to over 150 percent by 1927, while the bump relative to November grew from 65 to 90 percent over the decade. It is clear that Christmas has made an important dent in retail throughout the twentieth century.

How Much Did People Spend at Christmas?

In 2007 U.S. holiday spending was $66 billion and population was 302 million, so per capita holiday spending was $218. How large was per capita holiday spending sixty-five years earlier? The intervening generations had brought substantial economic growth. Per capita gross domestic product (GDP) grew from about $7,000 in 1935 to $35,000, with both measured in year 2000 dollars. That is, over this period of roughly three generations, income grew by a factor of five. (If you're looking for miracles, this growth rate is up there.) In 1935, U.S. holiday spending made up about $10 per million in GDP. Over the subsequent sixty-five years, this share fell steadily, reaching about $5 in 2000. In some sense, then, holiday spending loomed larger in 1935 than in 2000, since it took a larger share of total GDP.

But since GDP grew by a factor of seven, even though holiday spending's share of GDP fell by almost half, the overall amount of holiday spending essentially tripled, from about $75 per capita annually in the late 1930s to over $200 per year since 2000 (both in year 2007 dollars). Holiday spending was a bigger share of a smaller economy three generations ago. The economy has grown enormously since then, and while holiday giving has grown less explosively, it has still grown in absolute terms by about a factor of three.

The glass here is half empty and half full. In absolute (constant dollar) terms, our holiday retail spending has tripled. In that sense we are awful gluttons hastening Armageddon. But we've gotten more productive and richer over time, and the share of the economy that we devote to holiday spending has fallen by about half, reflecting a certain Calvinist thrift. Either way you look at it, though, the commercialization of Christmas in the United States is not new. As one observer noted, "There are worlds of money wasted, at this time of year, in getting things that nobody wants, and nobody cares for after they are got." The observer was the prescient Harriet Beecher Stowe, writing in 1850.

CHAPTER EIGHT

Have Yourself a Borrowed Little Christmas

As we've seen, the high volume of spending on Christmas is not a new phenomenon. But what about the way we pay for it? Americans have become debt junkies in the past half century. Has this changed the way we finance Christmas expenditures? And can we actually afford contemporary Christmas?

Remember "layaway"? How about "Christmas Club"? These are words not often heard these days, but they were once important retail institutions. Both allowed consumers to pay for Christmas gifts in advance of obtaining them, making them the polar opposite of today's preferred time pattern of buy now, pay later, using credit cards. Layaway programs allowed customers to reserve their desired items, pay when they could, then take the items home when they had paid in full (forgoing interest all the while on the money paid to the store). These programs had been a staple of shopping, particularly for low-income shoppers, and stores like Wal-Mart angered many of

these customers when they shuttered their layaway program in favor of more profitable store
credit cards. They may have acted too soon; the
Panic of 2007, and its ensuing credit crunch and
subsequent recession, paved the way for increased
demand for layaway plans at discount retailers
like Kmart, just in time for the 2008 Christmas
shopping season.

Christmas clubs, first offered by the Carlisle
Bank of Carlisle, Pennsylvania, in 1909, were
bank accounts in which customers could deposit
a little each week so they could afford presents
come Christmas. Of course, any account—or the
mattress—could serve this purpose. But just as
Odysseus had the foresight to tie himself to a
mast, some people appreciate help overcoming
their problems with self-discipline.

A 1927 scholarly treatment of Christmas club
accounts described their basic features. Members
promised to contribute weekly, frequently as
little as $0.25 per week. Accounts paid little in-
terest (1 or 2 percent rather than the 3 to 4.5
percent then available to depositors generally).
Around December 10, the banks disbursed the
savings to participants. The scholarly article at-
tributed the clubs' popularity to participant ignorance as well as the participants' understanding
that they lacked self-discipline: "The realization
on the part of many persons that they cannot,

without real or apparent compulsion, withstand the temptation to spend from time to time for unwarranted luxuries." Bank employees "and members of their families 'signed up' in Christmas clubs because they realized that otherwise the money would be 'frittered away.'" And, finally, the "Christmas club member promises to deposit a specified amount each week during the fifty-two week period. There is no legal compulsion, but there is a very real compulsion. It consists of suffering the disapprobation of the person in charge of the Christmas club if the pledge is not maintained." This despite the fact that "the person in charge is frequently only a very subordinate bank official."

Data on Christmas club accounts are scant, but the Federal Reserve reported Christmas club deposits, roughly quarterly, between the Depression years of 1933 and 1941. Sure enough, these deposits follow a "sawtooth" pattern. Deposits rise through the year, then fall at year-end. For example, Christmas club deposits stood at $18 million on December 31, 1933. In March of 1933 they had risen to $36 million. They climbed to $59 million in June; and in September (the last time we see their value before Christmas) they reached $80 million. Just after Christmas (December 31, 1934), they had fallen back to $19 million. It's likely that deposits continued to rise into early December, but we can conservatively say that consumers withdrew at least $61 million from Christmas club accounts—their October value less their value at New Year's—to buy Christmas gifts in 1934. Similarly, in 1935—the first year we have systematic retail sales data—the holiday withdrawals from Christmas club accounts were at least $63 million. Calculated by our usual method, Christmas spending totaled $647 million in 1935, so Christmas club savings financed about a tenth of Christmas in 1935. Prior to 1933 Christmas club accounts were tallied, along with other kinds of savings accounts, under "open accounts." These, too, fell substantially in each of the Decembers, by about $100 million in 1929 and by almost $300 million in 1930.

While Christmas clubs still exist, they are far less prominent than they once were. The reason, of course, is the widespread availability of consumer credit. For example, revolving credit—credit card debt—has grown from under $20 billion in 1970 to nearly a trillion dollars in 2008. Total consumer credit, including installment loans, stands at $2.5 trillion. Much of this trend growth is simply the growing use of credit cards rather than checks or cash for payment generally. Consumers regularly use credit cards at the gas station, the grocery store, and almost everywhere else. But apart from the trend growth in the use of credit cards as a payment mechanism, is there evidence of heavier reliance on debt at Christmas?

A comparison of nonseasonally adjusted retail sales and credit card debt for 2006 and 2007 is telling. Each series has a systematic annual pattern. Retail sales jump in December, then fall below their usual levels in January and February. Credit card debt has a strong upward trend over time, but it also has a seasonal pattern: it increases faster in November and even faster in December; then it actually coasts back toward its long upward trend in January and February. In March it has arrived back at the trend line it seemed to follow prior to Christmas. What does this tell us about how Christmas is financed?

Some consumers use their credit cards simply as charge cards. They charge their purchases, then pay them off within the month without incurring interest charges. The way the Fed calculates credit card debt, however, those consumers' balances appear as debt. So even if every user paid off her card the month she made the purchases, credit card debt would appear to swell each December (simply because of the high volume of sales and therefore of credit card charges). But debt isn't above trend only in December. Instead, it stays above trend in January and February as well, even though retail sales (and therefore new credit card charges) are well below normal in these months. This means that consumers are financing Christmas with debt paid off, typically, one to three months after the holiday.

We can roughly estimate how much of Christmas is debt-financed by comparing debt's excess, over its long-term trend in the months following Christmas, to that year's Christmas spending. We can calculate the monthly ratio of excess debt in December to holiday spending back to 1943. The share jumps around from year to year, but it averages about 40 percent between 1945 and 1980; then it rises from 40 to about 65 percent over the past twenty-five years. It looks as though two-thirds of annual holiday spending goes on plastic in December. Again, because credit cards are also charge cards, this does not necessarily reflect consumers taking on debt.

If consumers are actually taking on more debt—not simply charging more purchases— then their debt would remain above trend in January. Prior to 1980, the January ratio of excess debt relative to spending on the immediately preceding Christmas averaged about 15 percent. Since 1980 it has risen steadily to nearly 50 percent. That is, a month after Christmas, the holiday is now only halfway paid off. Of the component that was charged to credit cards in December, about three-quarters is not paid off.

82

83

February tells a similar story. Prior to 1980 there was no excess consumer debt in February. Since 1980 it has risen to 20 percent of preceding Christmas sales, or nearly a third of the amount going on the card in December. That is, a third of the money borrowed for Christmas spending is still not paid off two months after the holiday.

Although the volume of spending on Christmas was already high a few generations ago, the way we finance Christmas has changed substantially. Shoppers used to save up for Christmas, scrimping through the year so they could pay for their December splurge. The last thirty years have witnessed an explosion in the availability of credit. Shoppers now splurge in December and scrimp through a late-winter debt hangover.

Is Yuletide Borrowing Bad?

Many normal people would view Yuletide borrowing dimly, as yet another example of profligate American consumers living beyond their means. Because, of course, Americans do live beyond their means and consequently owe $584 billion to the Chinese for their inexpensive products, $170 billion to oil exporters for gasoline, and $504 billion to the Japanese for their cars and electronic toys. But debt is not necessarily bad. It's customary to borrow money to buy houses and cars, big-ticket items that generate a long-term service flow—and retain some value—long after they are purchased. It makes sense to borrow money to buy a house. If you waited until you had saved enough to get one, few people would live in houses until they were ready to retire. And durable assets (like houses or cars) are normally safe investments from a lender's perspective as well, since they retain value even if the borrower blows all his money at the track.

But most Christmas spending is for goods that are considerably less durable—and less easily resold—than housing or even cars, raising a question about whether it makes sense to go into hock for Christmas.

84

To an economist, the growth of credit—that is, the growth in the opportunities to borrow—is an unambiguously good development. Walking around with a credit line expands the set of opportunities that a consumer can seize. Maybe you'll encounter a great deal on something that is beyond your means today but inside your means next month. Access to credit allows you to take that advantage. Given that access to credit is helpful, it's hard to argue that the exercise of the option—to consume now and pay later, with interest—is bad.

85

That said, anything that you'd be embarrassed to tell your mother is probably not entirely good.

You, into the phone: "Mom, Wendy and I still owe a thousand on our Christmas presents." You listen and fidget; then you say: "Yes, I know it's February." You listen some more and squirm. "No, I haven't set up the kids' college funds yet." Mom: "Why couldn't you have saved up for Christmas? That's what Dad and I did when you were kids. You make a good living. Where does it all go?"

Mom's got a point. It's one thing to use credit to take advantage of an unexpected great deal that your future self can afford—and surely wants— even though your present self cannot. But it's another thing to borrow at 18 percent interest, rather than save, to pay for a fully anticipated expense. Christmas arrives on December 25 every year. It's fully anticipated by even dimly sentient beings. The need to begin spending the day after Thanksgiving does not come as a surprise. So why would a sensible person need to borrow for it?

True, there could be sensible strategic reasons to borrow to finance Christmas. One, from the Ronald Reagan playbook, is called "starve the beast." Reagan cut taxes even as he increased military spending as a cunning strategy to raise the federal deficit to the point that future "Democrat lawmakers"—the beast in this metaphor— would be forced to shrink the nonmilitary government. Translated to the domestic front, you and your spouse—the beast in the scenario—disagree on what to buy. You want a large new television, and your spouse wants a new roof. In November, you make the first move, and you charge a seventy-inch flat-screen television on the family credit card. Come January, you need to begin making payments. Because your family's income isn't going up, the only way to make ends meet is to not buy much of anything else. So your new TV crowds out the new roof. Beast starved. Maybe this is what explains American households' Yuletide borrowing. But if so, I think couples should sit down and talk more.

The more plausible explanation for this borrowing is what I call the "Homer Simpson theory of behavior." Why do people do things? According to Homer, "It's because they're stupid, that's why. That's why everyone does everything." Behavioral economics presents a similar theory using the more dignified, but equivalent, explanations that people procrastinate, have difficulty remembering what they like, and so on. Much of the use of credit by consumers at Christmas arises simply because, in short, they're as dumb as a box of hammers.

Skeptics need stronger evidence that Yuletide borrowing hurts borrowers to be convinced that the consumers are spending beyond their means. If consumers did terrible things to finance their

Christmas presents—selling their children or robbing people at gunpoint—even traditional economists would come around to conclude that Christmas was putting stress on their budgets. But borrowing at 18 percent is not quite homicide.

Does Christmas spending strain households to the breaking point? We get some evidence from the fringe of the financial world. "Payday lenders" are financial institutions that allow consumers to borrow against their next paycheck, at 18 percent for a loan lasting two weeks. That's an annual interest rate of about 7,300 percent. While it's possible that you might stumble across a buying opportunity so good that it's worth paying 7,000 percent annual interest, it seems more likely that this kind of borrowing follows some stupid and overextended spending.

And when does this kind of borrowing peak during the year? Shortly after Christmas. The volume of loan applications processed on January 2 is three times the volume on a typical day. Can we afford Christmas? Be honest. Remember, you're talking to your mom here. Let's just say that there's evidence of some strain on household finances produced by Yuletide borrowing.

CHAPTER NINE

*Is Christmas Like Spam,
Underwear, or Caviar?*

"What would I buy if I had more money?" is a common parlor game for middle-class Americans. For many, it's travel. For others, fancy cars or electronic toys. The television shows *Lifestyles of the Rich and Famous* and MTV's *Cribs* give viewers a glimpse of the material pleasures of wealth, providing a voyeuristic answer to the viewers' question "What would I buy if I had a lot more money?" If I were an uneducated nouveau riche athlete or musician, anyway. And we know from *Cribs* that hip, rich celebrities buy lots of fancy cars, as well as indoor basketball courts and gold-plated plumbing fixtures. *Cribs* is a great show, in the same sense that *Cops* and Mutual of Omaha's *Wild Kingdom* are great shows: you get to see how unfamiliar creatures live their lives—in this case, very rich creatures. But except for the comparison it affords with our own mundane consumption, couch-based social science does not allow a systematic comparison of consumption patterns across the entire income spectrum.

That requires—yawn—government statistics. While they are far less colorful—and a lot less specific—government statistics on spending give us a systematic answer to the question "What do people buy when they have more money?"

As people get richer, the amount of money they spend on some goods—Spam is the paradigmatic example—falls. Poor people buy a lot of Spam; rich people buy very little. So economists label these "inferior goods." For other goods, like underwear, while people buy more as they get richer, their expenditures do not keep up with their income, so the share of income allocated to the good falls. Food overall is the classic example. The negative relationship between income and food's share of expenditure is so regular that it is termed Engel's Law, after the German statistician who first noted it. While rich people spend more on underwear and food than do poor people, the proportion of the budget that the rich devote to underwear, and to food, falls short of the share devoted by the poor. Goods like underwear are "necessities." Finally, both the amount of money and the share of income spent on some goods actually rises as they get richer. Lobster, caviar, diamonds, and silk purses are examples of luxuries. So, what's Christmas? Spam, underwear, or caviar?

If buying stuff brings people satisfaction, then

knowing what additional stuff people would buy
if they had more money tells us what it is—mate-
rially anyway—that people aspire to have. Clearly,
we all need food, clothing, and shelter to survive.
But once these basic needs are taken care of,
what do people buy with whatever money they
have left? By studying what people buy as they
have more money, luxury voyeurism allows a
glimpse of what the rest of us would do if only we
had more money.

There are two broad ways to examine questions like this, over time and across people. We
have data over time in the United States, and we
have limited contemporary data on household
Christmas spending, allowing us to ask two specific questions. First, as the United States has gotten richer, has its Christmas spending increased
more or less than income? And how does our
changed Christmas spending compare with our
changed spending on major categories such as
food, clothing, shelter, medical care, and so on?
Second, as reflected by data on holiday spending
across households in the United States, do richer
households spend a larger share of their income
on Christmas?

As we saw earlier, the United States has gotten a great deal richer in the past few generations. As we have gotten richer, we have spent
more on Christmas. But Christmas spending in-

creased substantially less than income growth overall. This already suggests that Christmas is a necessity. But to make this comparison more accurately, we need to compare Christmas spending with other categories of expenditure. One source of information is personal consumption data from the National Income and Product Accounts (NIPA). Personal consumption is defined as "the value of the goods and services purchased by persons—that is, individuals, nonprofit institutions that primarily serve households, private non-insured welfare funds, and private trust funds." These data are available back to 1929, and they are broken into the following categories. First the nondurables: food, clothing, gasoline/fuel, and other nondurables. Then the durables: motor vehicles, furniture, and other. And finally the services: housing, household operation, transportation, medical care, recreation, and other services. There is, of course, some overlap between these categories of consumption and the measures of retail sales we've been using. Most nondurables and some durable goods (e.g., jewelry) are purchased at retail stores. But the services like housing and medical care are not generally available through retail outlets.

The question we can ask with these data is this: how did consumption in each category increase as income increased, between 1935 and

2007 (the years when we also have holiday spending data)? For each category, we'll summarize the relationship with a single number—which economists would call the elasticity of category spending with respect to total consumption –showing the percentage growth in the category with a percent growth in overall consumption. If this elasticity is 1, then the category maintains a constant share of consumption even as income grows. If the measure is positive but less than 1, the category shrinks as a share of consumption as income grows. Then the good is a necessity. And, finally, if the elasticity exceeds 1, the category grows as a share of consumption as total consumption grows, so the good is a luxury. Based on the relationship between the growth in the category and overall consumption over time, the categories with high elasticities are medical care, motor vehicles, and other durable goods. These are the only luxury categories, with elasticities above 1. At the other end of the spectrum, the categories with the lowest elasticities are food and clothing, at around 0.8.

How does Christmas spending stack up against these categories? It's just under 0.9, between food and gasoline. Against the backdrop of *Cribs*, it's a bit of a comedown to hear that Christmas has the glamour of the grocery store and the filling station.

92

93

We can also use contemporary data to determine which goods are luxuries and which are necessities. The Commerce Department conducts an ongoing survey of consumer expenditure to track changes in the price level. The survey also asks for household income, so it's easy to compare the share of expenditure devoted to each category for households with varying levels of income. As with the consumption data, we can summarize each category with an elasticity using data for 2006. Across households, the categories with elasticities above 1 include pensions, cash contributions to charity, education, entertainment, transportation, and alcohol. At the bottom end of the spectrum are health care, food, and housing, all between about 0.6 and 0.8. These two approaches agree on many of the overlapping categories. Food and clothing are clearly necessities in both sets of data. For example, poor households, with annual income below $5,000, allocate 15 percent of their expenditure to food and 39 percent to housing. At the other end of the spectrum, entertainment, cash contributions, and pensions are clearly luxury goods. While the poor allocate only 2 percent of their income to pensions, households with income above $150,000 allocate 15 percent of their income to pensions but only 11 and 32 percent to food and housing, respectively.

Imagine an episode of *Cribs* or *Lifestyles*.

"Here we are inside the home of John Q. Upper Middle Class." Let's say that John's family income is $300,000 per year, which puts them in the top percent of U.S. households. They are quite well off, although they're not rich enough for an indoor basketball court or gold-plated faucets. The host is puzzled. His usual well-off guests flaunt their material rewards. "So, John, what do you do with your money? This is a nice house, but looking around, I don't see where all those Benjamins are going, unless they're going up your nose."

John: "Well, MC DingDong, after we pay for food, clothing, and shelter, we put most of our remaining income into retirement savings and college for our kids. Oh, and we took a trip to Europe last year."

There you have it. High-income people spend a lot more than do average people on education and retirement savings. If we were trying to get clues about good gifts from what the rich do, then we should give people education and future consumption.

While the Consumer Expenditure Survey does not include a holiday giving category, other sources provide information on the relationship between holiday spending and household income. For example, the Gallup organization administers an annual spending survey to assess holiday spending. Between November 11 and 14, 2007, Gallup interviewed 1,014 adults and determined that American households planned to spend an average of $866 on Christmas gifts. Gallup reports Christmas spending plans in four ranges (under $250, $250–500, $500–1,000, over $1,000) separately for three categories of household income: under $30,000, between $30,000 and $75,000, and over $75,000. Using cell midpoints, we can get a rough sense of the relationship between Christmas spending and household income. Holiday gift expenditure clearly declines as income rises, and the implied income elasticity from the Gallup data is 0.3.

Two other polls, from the Conference Board and the Siena Research Institute, report similar data. Siena conducted a random phone survey of 570 residents of New York State between November 26 and 28, 2007, and reports holiday spending for seven household income categories. The Conference Board surveyed 5,000 households nationwide in November 2007 and reports holiday spending for five separate income categories. The Conference Board's average estimate was $471 in 2007. The implied income elasticities from these data are 0.3 and 0.5, respectively. It must be noted that these elasticities are not strictly comparable to the Consumer Expenditure Survey–based elasticities, since those are derived from the relationship between category and total expenditure, while these are based on the relationship between category expenditure and total income. Still, these clearly indicate that Christmas is a necessity. And not a particularly glamorous-looking one.

From a variety of approaches, it appears that Christmas is closer to being a necessity than it is to being a luxury. Christmas is like chicken or underwear. This is interesting and surprising by itself. It's also interesting when juxtaposed with information on another form of private giving, cash contributions.

As mentioned above, one of the expenditure categories in the Consumer Expenditure Survey is cash contributions. According to the BLS, "Cash contributions includes cash contributed to persons or organizations outside the consumer unit, including alimony and child support payments; care of students away from home; and contributions to religious, educational, charitable, or political organizations."

Based on the expenditure data, cash contributions have the second-highest elasticity, about 1.3, behind only pensions. Cash contributions are clearly a luxury, an activity that people would do more if they had more money. But Christmas giving is not. Christmas giving is something that people need to get out of the way, not something people wish they could do more of, if only they were richer. Christmas gift giving, pardon the metaphor, is a cross that we must bear.

Put this together with our finding on giver motivations in chapter 5, and we have a somewhat bleak view of Christmas. We are not prevented by our financial means from giving more, indicating that our giving is a necessity or an obligation, not an aspirational activity. On top of the obligation to give, we have a constraint against giving cash. Thanks a lot, Santa.

CHAPTER TEN

Christmas and Commercialism:
Are Santa and Jesus on the Same Team?
If So, Who's Team Captain?

A Seattle-area resident named Art Conrad, feeling that "Santa has been co-opted by our corporations as a symbol of consumerism," and that "[e]very year Christmas comes earlier and earlier," got fed up and erected Santa-on-the-cross in his yard to protest commercialization during the run-up to Christmas 2007. Art Conrad is not alone in his dismay at Christmas; Yuletide dissidents tend to display their concern over the excessive commercialism of Christmas in one of two ways. In one corner we have Art Conrad, the pope, environmentalists, and various Protestants condemning massive consumption at Christmas that, variously, distracts people from the true meaning of the holiday and destroys the planet. In the opposing corner we have the Religious Right, annoyed that retailers have banished Jesus from the mall.

The pope made a media splash in 2005. In his weekly Angelus (media address) in St. Peter's Square, "Pope Benedict XVI chided the increased commercialism surrounding Christmas, and stressed the importance of Nativity scenes in family homes. He began his address before the prayer by criticizing 'today's consumer society' saying that because of it, the Christmas season 'suffers from the "contamination" of commercialism that risks changing its true spirit, characterized by reflection, sobriety and a joy that does not come from outside, but from within.'"

An organization called New American Dream, whose mission is "to help Americans consume responsibly to protect the environment, enhance quality of life, and promote social justice," launched a campaign to "simplify the holidays." They envision an ideal holiday that "would include the company of loved ones, good food, fun and relaxation . . . maybe an inch or two of snow. . . . [W]e might even envision a feeling of tranquility and peace blanketing our homes, our community, the wide world."

This ideal stands in contrast "with the typical mid-December scene at the mall, where countless holiday shoppers weave between traffic, oscillating between oppressed weariness and panic, as they search for non-existent parking spaces and that perfect gift that says 'I had no earthly idea what to get you, but chose this particular item because, um, it is shiny and appears to cost what I could reasonably be expected to spend.'"

Their concerns continue: "[T]he holidays, meant to be a time of peace, reflection, and celebration, too often exhaust rather than uplift us. If you sometimes feel trapped by the shopping, spending, crass displays, and frenzied preparations, you aren't alone. Our national surveys consistently show that Americans feel put upon by the commercialization of the season and want more of what matters . . . not just more stuff."

And even a Protestant-based financial planning organization ("God is using Crown Financial Ministries around the globe to teach His financial principles and transform lives") criticizes excessive commercialism at Christmas. According to Crown CEO Howard Dayton, "Christmas is celebrated today more as a sales frenzy than as the most important birth in history. Unfortunately, Christians are susceptible to this commercial mentality, and too many have compromised the message of giving. Often, we give useless gifts at Christmas, because it's expected of us, and we feel guilty if we don't. And the closer we get to Christmas, the pressure to give these unnecessary gifts builds and we feel depressed and unworthy if we can't give."

The pope, a Baptist financial planner, and the tree huggers agree, in short, that there's too much commercialism in Christmas, or that Jesus would like to distance himself from Santa.

Now to the opposing corner: weighing in at eight hundred pounds, and resembling a gorilla, we have Fox News and vocal elements of the Religious Right whose concern is *not* that there's too much commercialism in Christmas but rather the opposite: *that there's not enough Christianity* in the commercial sphere.

Over the past few years, many retailers have come to believe that not all of their customers wish to be bid a "Merry Christmas." In their advertising and store decorations they have retreated to less religiously specific exhortations such as "Happy Holidays." And while advertising and displays emphasize red-and-green color schemes and may feature reindeer or even Santa Claus, major stores shy away from Nativity scenes or even "Merry Christmas." This alarms some, such as the American Family Association (AFA), which, according to their mission statement, "exists to motivate and equip citizens to change the culture to reflect Biblical truth." Strategically, the AFA believes "in holding accountable the companies which sponsor programs attacking traditional family values."

Accordingly, the AFA orchestrated a boycott of Target for "not using the words 'Merry Christmas' in its advertising." And Fox News anchor Bill O'Reilly orchestrated a "Christmas Under Siege" campaign, with a chart on his Web site of stores that use the phrase "Happy Holidays," along with a poll that asks, "Will you shop at stores that do not say 'Merry Christmas'?" This campaign received attention on both Fox and conservative talk radio.

Bill O'Reilly and the AFA have no quarrel with commercialism in Christmas. Commercialism is fine. Their problem is that religion—Jesus in particular—is absent from the mall.

The criticism leveled in this book is neither of the above, although it is closer to the first concern—excessive consumption. But to be clear, my beef is not with the level of spending and consumption at Christmas but rather with the waste this spending generates. Gift giving matches resources poorly with users, producing a meager amount of material satisfaction for the amount of money spent. It's probably wrong to pillage the planet in celebration of Christmas. But if pillage we must, we should at least do it efficiently.

CHAPTER ELEVEN

Stop Carping; It's All for the Best

In Voltaire's *Candide*, Dr. Pangloss is an inveterate optimist and a precursor to the economic Pollyannas who see only the best in whatever happens. One might, for example, view the common human need for vision correction as a pathology. But for Dr. Pangloss, the status quo is all for the best: noses are proof that humans were intended to wear spectacles. Throughout *Candide*, despite many obstacles, Dr. Pangloss maintains that "all is for the best in this best of all possible worlds." Voltaire conceived Pangloss as a device for mocking optimists such as the followers of the philosopher Leibniz, who believed that an omnipotent and benevolent God created this world as the "best of all possible worlds." (Leibniz also invented calculus, leading generations of high school students to question how benevolent this God actually was.)

Some people doubt that the waste I identify is actually waste at all. Their arguments, recalling Dr. Pangloss, go like this:

1. Christmas giving among private individuals is voluntary, and whatever people do voluntarily cannot, by definition, be inefficient. Rather, it's all for the best . . .

2. People have been giving Christmas gifts, in their current form, for most of the last century—and do so throughout the developed world. An institution so durable could not possibly be inefficient. If it were, it would have gone away already. It must be all for the best . . .

Let's explore these interesting arguments.

Christmas Giving Is Voluntary and
Therefore Perforce Good

In its simplest form, the idea is this. If a consumer faces a choice among many pieces of fruit, each costing a dollar, and he chooses the apple, he must prefer apples. We can infer from his choice that apples deliver him more satisfaction than do the alternatives. When choice is not constrained—whenever people are "free to choose," to quote Milton Friedman—people's choices indicate what is best for them.

So it is with Christmas giving. If givers freely choose to purchase gifts for their recipients, then giving gifts—and giving those gifts in particular—is the choice that delivers the givers the greatest possible satisfaction. Just as our noses were made to hold spectacles, givers were intended to buy gifts that others do not want. We know this because they do it. *Quod erat demonstrandum.*

The keys to the proof that the status quo is ideal are the notions that (a) the giver is free to choose among alternatives, and (b) the giver is informed about the consequences of his decision for his recipient's satisfaction. I'll address (b) below, so let's concentrate on (a).

At the risk of channeling Bill Clinton's slipperiest moment, whether we are free not to give holiday gifts depends on what the definition of "free" is. For example, I'm not free to ignore my income tax bill. If I don't pay it, after a lengthy process of delivering me warnings and subpoenas, the IRS will send agents with guns and handcuffs to my house to cart me off to jail.

On the other hand, if I do not purchase a gift for my mother, nobody—not the IRS, the Bureau of Alcohol, Tobacco, and Firearms, the FBI, nor even the local police—will come after me with guns. I cannot be thrown in jail for failing to buy Mom a gift. In that sense I am free to choose stiffing Mom at the holidays.

But am I? Are laws the only relevant restrictions on human behavior? Are we really free to do anything that is not proscribed by law? This is important, because if our choices are not made freely, then we cannot infer optimality from choice.

Is there a doctor of sociology in the house? Like economists, sociologists are concerned with why people do what they do ("action"), and what happens when they—and others—do ("order"). For reasons of tradition and perhaps predilection, economists emphasize freedom to choose, while sociologists emphasize social norms—constraints on behavior outside of individuals—as explanations of individual behavior. While economists assume that people can make any choice they can afford—perhaps except those that are illegal—a sociologist sees a narrower range of choices, constrained by social norms.

Why are there particular behaviors that most people avoid at a cost of personal inconvenience, even though they are not expensive or illegal? For example, why don't professors belch or pass gas during their lectures? There's no law against either behavior, at least none that's enforced.

And why do so many people behave similarly even without a similar coincidence of individual benefit? Why do we usually arrange to meet for lunch at noon? Why do Westerners use forks, knives, and napkins to facilitate eating? Why do we set the table with the fork on the left and the knife on the right? And so on. These are all what sociologists term "normative" behaviors. We adopt them because we "are supposed to," not because it serves our individual interests to do so, at least in those particular ways.

I am legally free to set the table differently. And I am legally free to belch while teaching college students. But I do not, nor does anyone I know. We are also all legally free not to give Christmas presents.

What happens if I violate a behavioral norm? Well, if I belched in front of the class, the first time students would giggle. The second time, they would squirm nervously and talk ill of me after class. If I did it on a third occasion, they would openly express their disapproval, and warnings to future students would start showing up on my RateMyProfessors.com page.

So I do face sanctions—albeit not jail—for violating social norms. Unless we've all agreed in advance not to exchange gifts, if I come to the big holiday gathering empty-handed, my behavior will earn me the enmity of my relatives.

I ask again: are we free not to give gifts at Christmas? My best answer is somewhere between "sort of" and "no." If we are not free to choose not to give gifts, then the givers' choice to give does not reveal that giving was ideal, nor even that it was better than not giving. Instead, we do it because this is the way we do it, like the way we set the table.

In the formerly authoritarian Soviet Union, voting was mandatory even though only one candidate—the Communist Party nominee—appeared on the ballot. After elections the Party would trumpet the winner's landslide victory—nearly 100 percent of the vote!—as evidence of the people's enthusiasm. And looky here: Comrade Santa also has 95 percent of the vote!

How Could Inefficient Christmas Giving Persist?

108

When bad things happen to good people, economists tend to look for diagnoses involving misaligned incentives. If people follow their self-interest, and this pursuit generally works out for the best, then if something goes wrong, a good guess is that people faced the wrong incentives, as when an employee—George Jetson—does not act in the best interest of the company owner, Cosmo G. Spacely, boss of Spacely Sprockets. This is the paradigmatic example of what economists term a "principal-agent problem."

Cosmo is trying to motivate George to work hard, which will—probably—make Spacely Sprockets more profitable. George's effort is hard to monitor, but in the end Cosmo knows whether George succeeded at his task, which is more likely if George exerted concerted effort. But working hard is onerous, and George could always defect to crosstown competitor Cogswell Cogs, so getting George to work hard requires compensation. Here's where it gets interesting. Cosmo can offer George some mix of base pay, paid regardless of how well the firm does, and bonus, paid only if the firm does well, which—again—is more likely but not certain if George works hard.

Clearly, relying more on bonus pay provides stronger incentives for George to work hard. But if George is like most people, he does not enjoy the risk that comes with heavy reliance on bonus pay. He prefers a large base, which guarantees his income but—to Cosmo's chagrin—provides no incentive for George to exert effort.

What's Cosmo to do? Presumably, he experiments with combinations of base and bonus pay until he finds one that balances the profitability benefit of stronger incentives against the ulcer-inducing risk-bearing costs that George must experience.

What does this have to do with Christmas, you ask? I am claiming that, with Christmas giving, bad things are repeatedly happening to good people. This can occur—persistently—if givers face misaligned incentives. Can we shed any light on this problem by casting holiday gift giving in the principal-agent framework?

Yes! Think of a child as the principal—the boss of the kid's get-me-what-I-want enterprise—and Grandma as the agent, the lackey employed to implement the kid's whims. The child—Tommy—wants Grand Theft Auto IV™. Grandma, however, has no clue. She searches high and low for an appropriate present. (*A board game? A medicine ball? What did we like as kids in the 1940s? Yes, a kaleidoscope!*) How could this kind of behavior persist in Grandma, year after year?

Well, Grandma does not face strong incentives. The gift-giving institution would do a better job at delivering Tommy what he wants if Grandma got a sharp stick in the eye for giving a kid a kaleidoscope, or if Christmas morning unfolded like this: Picture a warm family scene, with three generations of the family in bathrobes and slippers, adults sipping coffee, kids sipping hot chocolate. The kids, who went to church last night, have been awake since 5:30 a.m., eager to open their presents. Fast forward to Tommy opening Grandma's present. "*Grand Theft Auto, Grand Theft Auto, Grand Theft Auto,*" Tommy says silently to himself, fingers crossed. He eagerly removes the wrapping from the wrong-shaped-box-but-that's-OK-'cause-Grandma-probably-rewrapped-it. He opens the box and begins to worry. (Reminder: we're imagining a world in which Grandma faces sharp incentives, so what follows is not for the fainthearted.)

Tommy sees what's in the box and flies into a rage. "A friggin' kaleidoscope? What the heck were you thinking, you old bat? I hate this thing, and I hate you."

Snap to. Of course, this is not what Tommy says. He musters a smile and says, "Thanks, Grandma. I love you." She's not stupid. She doubts she got what he really wanted. But she doesn't get feedback that is proportionate to the size of her gift-giving faux pas. So she doesn't face compelling incentives to improve next year.

And let's be clear: Tommy's muted reaction is as it should be. We would all be very disappointed if Tommy said what he was thinking at the moment of his painful disappointment. We've trained him for this type of moment, and he passed. Frankly, his parents passed too. But the way we socialized him helps perpetuate the wastefulness of Christmas gifts.

The fact that civilized behavior precludes giving Grandma the incentives to deliver high-yield gifts means that, yes, Virginia, we can keep giving until it hurts the economy for a long time.

CHAPTER TWELVE

*Making Giving More Efficient
with Cash and Gift Cards*

Nature abhors a vacuum, and the economy—am I projecting here?—abhors waste. So, as we've seen, older and distant relatives have always gotten special dispensation allowing them to give cash without creating feelings of awkwardness. And because so much money is on the line, custom has traditionally allowed newlyweds to specify precisely what they want, through wedding registries, effectively turning all gifts into cash. But what about the rest of our giving? Where's the special dispensation allowing the common man to give cash? It's come in the form of gift cards.

While handwritten gift certificates have existed for a long time, present-day electronic gift cards really took off in the late 1990s. It is ironic, given the limited appeal of gasoline as a gift, that Mobil Oil issued the first gift card, in 1995. Within a few years the gift card concept caught on widely. Gift card sales reached $12 billion in 1998 and have grown steadily—averaging 27 percent per year—to 2005, when they reached $63 billion. In the past few years they have continued to grow.

Why have gift card sales grown so much in the past ten years? Jennifer Pate Offenberg suggests a few explanations: the growth of national chains, along with harried gift givers, particularly women, who lack time to shop for more specific items. Perhaps most important, the stigma attached to gift cards has eroded. The very repetitiveness with which this development has been heralded testifies to the power of the disapprobation that gift cards once drew. In a 2006 National Public Radio report: "That stigma is gone away." The Wilkes-Barre *Citizen's Voice* in 2006: "Gift Cards Lose Stigma." According to a National Retail Federation spokesman in 2007, "The stigma of it not being as personal as it could be has really started to diminish." Such sentiments were commonplace in 2007: "The stigma of gift cards is disappearing."

And, in another reflection of the eroded stigma, givers know that recipients really want gift cards. In 2007 gift cards were at or near the top of the list of most-wanted gifts. In a National Retail Federation survey, "gift cards were the No. 1 most-wished for item, above apparel and books and CDs." Gift cards came in second in a Consumer Reports most-wished-for survey, behind only clothing. In an American Express survey, gift cards were third, "behind clothes and CDs/DVDs."

The eminent and clever economist Bob Solow once quipped that computers were everywhere except in the productivity statistics. That was 1987; since then computers have made important cameos in the productivity statistics. Gift cards, too, seem ubiquitous, especially around the holidays. Is there any evidence of them in the retail sales statistics?

When retailers sell a one-hundred-dollar gift card, although they take your money right away, they do not recognize revenue from the transaction. Instead, the retailers incur a liability—they must stand ready to give the card holder a hundred dollars' worth of merchandise. The retailer records revenue only when the holder redeems the card. Importantly, the government statistics work the same way. Sales to gift card holders appear in the retail sales statistics at redemption. The majority of gift cards—perhaps 80 percent—are redeemed in January, and gift cards bring enough shoppers to the stores in January that a month previously reserved for markdowns and closeouts has been rechristened "a hot month for retail." If gift cards have been growing as a share of Christmas gift spending, then we should see a growth in January retail sales—when cards are redeemed—relative to December sales, when cards, rather than particular items, are purchased. The retail sales falloff between December and January should have shrunk since about 1997, and the falloff should have shrunk more in the retail categories where gift cards are most prominent: apparel, books, department stores, and perhaps discounters as well. Is it so?

The proportionate drop-off between December and January fluctuates year to year. In recession years such as 1974, with disappointing holiday spending seasons, the drop-off is small. Except for 1974, when it fell to 21 percent, between 1967 and 1995 the proportionate drop-off fluctuated between 23 and 30 percent. The drop-off reached 25 percent in 1999 and has fallen to unprecedented levels since: 20 percent in 2002 and 19 percent in 2007. The recent drop-off for general merchandise stores is even more pronounced. In short, gift cards are visible in the retail sales statistics.

From the standpoint of consumer theory, gift cards are an encouraging development, with the promise to greatly reduce Christmas waste. My always-supportive wife believes that my work and its public exposure in the early to mid-1990s helped propel the gift card trend. At least that's what she tells me.

But there's a catch. Roughly a tenth of gift

card value is never redeemed. People forget about their cards, or lose them, or they redeem part but then can't find something they want that costs less than the remaining balance, or the store issuing the card goes bankrupt. For whatever reason, about $8 billion per year goes unredeemed.

What happens to this money? Based on a rapidly developing body of historical experience, stores have determined that after about four years, unredeemed balances are likely never to be redeemed. So after, say, four years, stores "recognize" unredeemed gift card balances as revenue. They typically do this quietly, and information about the process is hard to come by. According to a 2006 newspaper account, "Target Corp., the second-largest U.S. discount retailer, records a percentage of each gift-card sale as revenue at the time the card is sold based on an estimate of the amount that won't be redeemed, spokeswoman Cathy Wright said. She wouldn't say what the percentage is or how much it added to sales." And "Wal-Mart Stores Inc., the world's largest retailer, doesn't provide any information on its policy for unused gift cards, spokesman Marty Heires said." When they have come to light, some of these recognitions have created bad publicity. It was widely reported that Home Depot recognized $43 million in unredeemed cards as revenue in 2006.

116

117

The prospect of boosting bottom lines with unredeemed cards is not lost on corporate financial officers. An article in *CFO Magazine* entitled "Re-gifting: Unused Cards Can Boost Company Income" was subtitled, "As Black Friday approaches, people will be spending billions on gift cards. Many companies will profit from those who lose them." Enough said.

A number of states, including Delaware, claim unredeemed gift card balances under unclaimed property laws. In those cases it's taxpayers rather than, say, Home Depot shareholders who get a piece of your recipients' gift cards. Regulators have started scrutinizing gift cards, and some states prohibit gift card expiration. Others compel retailers to redeem balances below $10 for cash.

So for every dollar a giver spends on a gift certificate, the recipient gets an average of only ninety cents. Viewed as a way to transfer satisfaction from giver to recipient, this is not much better than typical gift giving. There is one important difference, although it will provide cold comfort to givers. From a purely economic standpoint, giving money to the Gap, or Target, or Macy's is not value destruction; it's just a transfer. A transfer that the giver did not intend, but a transfer nonetheless.

When I buy you a $100 lamp, its manufacture

and distribution required something like $100 in real resources. If you value it at only $50, we're getting $50 in value out of something that required $100 to make. It's clearly value destruction. Compare that to a situation in which I give you a $100 gift card, and you redeem only half of it. Then you get at least $50 in satisfaction. The other $50 is not destroyed. Target Corporation distributes it to shareholders, who buy whatever they want with it. Yes, Target shareholders are people too, and bless you for thinking of them this time of year. I bet you didn't even know they were on your gift list. You're not on theirs.

Although they are technically "efficient," gift cards are disappointingly ineffective as tools for transferring satisfaction from the giver to his or her intended recipient. While they are an encouraging development, they don't let Santa off the hook. (In chapter 14 I'll return to gift cards with an idea for making giving better.)

CHAPTER THIRTEEN

Giving and Redistribution

Gifts from those with plenty to those with little can increase society's net satisfaction. This stems from a fundamental idea of economics, that as you get more of something, you get tired of it. The idea, called "declining marginal utility," can be amusingly illustrated with a bunch of bananas and a willing volunteer. Indeed, I do this exercise every year in my Wharton class after finding a volunteer who is still willing to participate after learning that the subject must like bananas, must not embarrass easily, and must have eaten breakfast that morning. "Come to the front of the classroom. Take a bite of the first banana, and tell me—on a 1-to-10 scale—how much you enjoy it." He—and the volunteer is usually male—takes a bite, chews, while the class laughs nervously. He usually rates the first bite a 10. Ditto for the second bite. And the third. Around the fourth bite, the rating falls, to 9 or 8. By the middle of the second banana, the bites rate a 6. The student is usually surprised when I instruct him to begin the third banana. By the end of the third banana, the ratings have fallen to 2 or 3. After a few bites of the fourth banana, the rating falls to zero, and I have to pay him a nickel or perhaps a quarter to take another bite.

The last bite confers no benefit on the volunteer. Compare that stuffed volunteer with another student who missed breakfast. How much would the hungry student have enjoyed the banana bite compared with the stuffed student? It's easy to say that the amount of happiness in the room would have been higher if the hungry student had taken the bite instead of the stuffed student. Given that people get sick of bananas when they have a lot—what I'll call the "banana effect"—an omniscient social planner trying to make a group of people as happy as possible would spread them around. Any time your next bite contributes more to happiness than my last bite, we'd get happier as a group if I gave you my last bite. If we all get tired of bananas at the same rate, then our collective happiness reaches its greatest level with an equal distribution of bananas.

Of course we get sick of bananas. But bananas aren't the coin of the realm. Money is. Do people get tired of money? After all, when I tire of bananas, I can start buying yachts. And when I grow weary of yachts, I can buy diamonds. And so on.

But here, too, one can imagine arraying a person's possible purchases from the most to least satisfying, per dollar spent. As long as the next thing I would purchase generates more satisfaction than the last thing you would purchase, we get better off if you give me some of what's yours.

Of course, this comparison—of my satisfaction against yours—is difficult, some would say impossible. If you have food left on your plate but you are literally sated, then—as long as food is not storable—we are better off if I get your plate leavings. That is, I am better off, and you are no worse off. But this is an extreme hypothetical example. Usually, we would each derive some additional benefit from each of the things on my plate. So comparing my benefit against yours would challenge even wise King Solomon.

One resolution of this problem comes from the voluntary decision of some people to part with what they deem their excess. Ted Turner surprised the world in 1997 when he pledged a billion-dollar charitable gift to the UN. "There are so many rich guys in the world, billionaires," explained Turner. "The world is awash in money and nobody knows what to do with it." He planned to goad other billionaires into doing their part. "We don't want the money they know what to do with, just the money they don't know what to do with." Ted had enough money so that he couldn't find anything interesting to get for himself with his last billion. If the UN could find something useful to do with it, giving it to them—and to its ultimate beneficiaries—could make the world better off.

As impressive as Turner's gift was, it was dwarfed three years later when Bill and Melinda Gates gave $16 billion to their foundation, set up to fund health initiatives in Africa and education around the world. As of 2006, the Gates Foundation had disbursed over $8 billion. That Ted Turner and the Gates family voluntarily gave up billions suggests that the marginal utility of money, like bananas, also declines.

If we all had an identical schedule mapping our personal resources to our personal happiness, then if we all had declining marginal utility—we all experienced the banana effect—King Solomon could easily maximize social happiness with an equal distribution of resources. This may underlie the reflexive notion that equal divisions of pie, literal and metaphorical, are "fair." To see this clearly, suppose you have a lot and I have only a little. Compare the satisfaction produced by the last morsel each of us has. Mine is high, since I have only a little already. Yours is low because you have a lot. If you gave me that morsel, you'd lose only a little satisfaction while I'd gain a lot. So on net, we're better off if you give me some when you have more than I. Of course, you're not better off. You're worse off, but you're worse off by less than the improvement to my well-being. This logic continues until we each have the same amount of stuff, so that an additional morsel could confer the same benefit on each of us. We call this division fair, but it would also be efficient if our preferences were identical and followed the banana principle.

The idea of redistribution doesn't sit well with some people. First off, if you take property rights seriously, then forcibly taking money from me to support you is a kind of theft. Indeed, this is the main argument that libertarians have leveled at government redistribution for decades. Hands off what's mine. Or, from the Cato Institute: "A progressive income tax violates the very heart and soul of the Framer's Constitution of liberty." Why? Because "[o]ur constitutional democracy rests on the principles that individuals are equal under the law, that consent is the basis of just laws, and that the powers of the federal government are strictly limited. None of those principles are consistent with taxing incomes at progressively higher rates."

Despite the difficulties with interpersonal comparisons, the banana principle—or its "fairness" implication favoring equal division—underlies public policy in many countries, most notably through the progressive structure of income taxation. In the United States and many other developed countries, not only are higher-income people required to pay more of their income in taxes, they also pay a higher *share* of their income as taxes. In the United States, if you're married, filing jointly with your spouse, you pay 10 percent on the first $15,000 in taxable income, 15 percent on the income between $15,000 and $63,000, 25 percent on the income from $63,000 to $129,000, 33 percent on the income from $129,000 to $350,000, and 35 percent thereafter. Thus a family making $40,000 in adjusted gross income would pay 13 percent, or $5,200, in federal taxes, while a family making $400,000 would pay 23.7 percent of its income, or nearly $95,000, in federal taxes. The second family pays almost twenty times more in taxes despite having only—only!—ten times the income. Progressive taxes are the banana principle in action. The idea is to minimize the pain of taxes by imposing more on the rich, whose marginal dollars are like twenty-seventh bites of bananas and can be forgone with little pain, than on the poor, whose marginal dollars are like the first few bites of bananas and are precious to them. In the past fifty years the U.S. tax system has become less steeply progressive. In the 1950s the top income tax rate was 91 percent; in the 1960s it fell to 70 percent, and it's now 35 percent. But the structure remains progressive.

The world distribution of income is very unequal, giving some scope for redistribution via the banana principle to increase world well-being. World population in 2006 was around 6.3 billion, and world GDP was about $47.5 trillion in U.S. dollars. The simple average per capita world income—total world income divided by world population—was therefore $7,500 per year. Not rich, but not terrible. A four-person household would have an income of $30,000, about what two people would make before taxes working full-time at $7.50 per hour.

A simple average describes the situation of a typical person if everyone has the same income, or, to a lesser extent, if the distribution of incomes is symmetric. Then the mean (or simple average) is the same as the median (the income of the middle person, when people are ordered from highest to lowest). As it turns out, however, world income is highly skewed toward a few rich countries, so the mean income does not describe a typical Earthling's income at all.

Ten of the poorest countries in the world are the sub-Saharan African nations of Burundi ($111 in per capita annual GDP), Democratic Republic of Congo ($141), Ethiopia ($173), Liberia ($176), Guinea-Bissau ($185), Eritrea ($231), Malawi ($233), Sierra Leone ($252), Rwanda ($263), and Niger ($267). Collectively, these countries have a population of about 200 million people and total GDP of $35.6 billion, for an average per capita GDP of $180. These aren't the only low-income countries in the world. Low income is the rule rather than the exception.

The populations of the bottom 20 percent of countries—roughly 1.2 billion people—have 2 percent of world income. The bottom 40 percent of countries in population have 4 percent of world income. The bottom 60 percent have 10 percent, and the bottom 80 percent have 20 percent. This, of course, means that the top 20 percent have 80 percent of world income. The average income in the top group is forty times the average per capita income in the bottom group.

It's not hard to see a potential application of the banana principle here. If a dollar in the hands of a poor person does more good than a dollar in the hands of a rich person, then redistribution from rich to poor countries could make the world better off. But even if you're willing to share, there's an active debate over whether aid helps its recipients. For example, William Easterly argues that the West has little to show for sizable foreign aid expenditures to foster the development of poor countries over the years. Jeff Sachs, on the other hand, argues that the West has an opportunity to transform the developing world and end poverty forever.

Resolving this debate is beyond the scope of this book. But there is reason to think that there are some worthwhile redistributive projects. The work of the Copenhagen Consensus provides some examples. The Copenhagen Consensus, organized by Bjørn Lomborg, seeks to answer the following questions: "Imagine you had $75 billion to donate to worthwhile causes. What would you do, and where should we start?" To this end, the group commissions studies by experts on the world's pressing problems. The studies are presented to a tough audience including Nobel Prize–winning economists, who brainstorm for a week to assemble a prioritized list of projects with high social return.

In 2008 their top priority, for example, was "Combating malnutrition in the 140 million children who are undernourished." The plan calls for "providing micronutrients for 80% of the 140 million children who lack essential vitamins in the form of vitamin A capsules and a course of zinc supplements," and "would cost just $60 million per year . . . this action holds yearly benefits of more than $1 billion. In effect, this means that each dollar spent on this program creates benefits (in the form of better health, fewer deaths, increased future earnings, etc.) worth more than 17 dollars."

Their prioritized list has many additional projects, including "implement[ing] the DOHA development plan" and "micronutrient fortification involving the iodization of salt and fortification of basic food items with iron."

Moving some of Ted Turner's extra billions—and maybe even some of yours—to these projects could easily make the world better off. If so, it could produce more benefit for recipients than it costs the givers.

Talk of redistribution makes some nervous because the utilitarian rationale for giving—that we can make the world better off by taking from the rich to give to the poor—smacks of communism's motto, "From each according to his ability, to each according to his need." Appeals for redistribution along these lines have all the appeal of Soviet-bloc consumer goods. Have you driven a Trabant lately? If economies based, at least ostensibly, on this kind of sharing were successful, then perhaps the club of communist countries would have a more inspiring membership roster than North Korea and Cuba.

Fortunately, the success of communism is not the most compelling argument in favor of redistribution toward worthy causes and the poor. First, people give voluntarily. And not just the likes of Ted Turner and Bill Gates. According to the National Center for Charitable Statistics, Americans who itemized charitable contributions on their tax return gave $166 billion to charity in 2005. Total U.S. private giving has been estimated elsewhere at $261 billion for 2005. If giving is happening, then while there's no guarantee that doing so is perfect or natural, it is clearly not necessary to train guns on people to induce them to share their resources.

Individuals aren't the only ones giving to the poor. People also give via the foreign aid budgets of their governments. According to the OECD, the United States gave $23.5 billion in foreign aid in 2006, the largest contribution of any country. Contributions from twenty-two major countries together totaled $104 billion. Other large contributors included the United Kingdom ($12.5 billion), Japan ($11.2), France ($10.6), and Germany ($10.4).

As a share of national income, however, the U.S. contribution was among the smallest, ahead of only Greece. Sweden's foreign aid contribution was just over a percent of gross national income, and other northern European countries (Norway, Luxembourg, the Netherlands, and Denmark) were not far behind, around 0.8 percent of income. The United States, by contrast, gave 0.18 percent, under half of the average country effort of 0.46. Like all countries outside northern Europe, the United States falls short of the UN giving target of 0.7 percent of national income for foreign aid. The United States was more generous with grants of foreign aid from private voluntary agencies, giving a total of $9 billion in 2006, or an additional 0.068 percent of national income, behind only Ireland, Canada, Switzerland, and Australia.   130

So resources are transferred from richer to poorer countries and people, voluntarily. Perhaps   131
more interesting than the fact that these transfers are voluntary is the fact that giving is a luxury activity, like golfing in Palm Springs or sipping vintage Champagne. We saw this clearly in the U.S. expenditure data in chapter 9. Not only do high-income households in the United States give absolutely more to charity than do their lower-income counterparts; the rich actually give a much higher percentage of their income. That is, the share of expenditure going to charity rises with income, making charitable giving one of the few broad categories of expenditure (along with

pension saving and recreational activity) that behave like textbook luxuries. Giving is something people would do if they had more money.

The foreign aid data also provide evidence that giving is a luxury. Only the wealthiest countries appear on the giving list at all. And among rich countries—except for the United States—the richer ones tend to give a larger share of income as foreign aid.

Redistribution provides a beneficial double whammy. First, moving resources from rich to poor benefits the poor more than it costs the rich, via the banana principle. Second, no guns are required; that is, we see a substantial amount of voluntary giving, within and between countries. Indeed, not only are people willing to give, they also treat giving as a luxury.

What does this have to do with Christmas, you may ask? What if we could find a way to enable our Christmas gift recipients to do something they'd like to do—give to charity—and at the same time do something good for the world? Did you hear the one about the two richest guys in the world? In 2006 the world's second richest man decided to give the world's richest family a gift. What did Warren Buffet give to Bill and Melinda Gates? He pledged about $30 billion in Berkshire Hathaway stock to the Gates Foundation. Asked by *Fortune* magazine, "Does it occur to you that it's somewhat ironic for the second-richest man in the world to be giving untold billions to the first-richest man?" Buffett answered, "When you put it that way, it sounds pretty funny. But in truth, I'm giving it *through* him . . . not to him." We can't all be Warren Buffett or Bill Gates. But many of us can give charitable gifts *through* our friends and loved ones.

CHAPTER FOURTEEN

*Solutions—Making Gift Giving
a Force for Good*

OK, Mr. Smart-Guy economist. They don't call it the "dismal science" for nothing. Thanks a lot for ruining Christmas. Do you at least have any sage advice?

I do, but before offering it, I am reminded of an old joke about European stereotypes: "Heaven is a place where the police are English; the chefs are Italian; the car mechanics are German; the lovers are French; and it's all organized by the Swiss. Hell is a place where the police are German; the chefs are English; the car mechanics are French; the lovers are Swiss; and it's all organized by the Italians." Taking gift-giving advice from an economist is a little like taking a Swiss lover. If you really want to give gifts, you should probably trust your instincts rather than a curmudgeonly economist you've never met.

That said, here's the hand we've been dealt. We have to buy gifts, and we can't give cash. We have to buy for a lot of people, ranging from people we know intimately to those we don't know at all. Deloitte Touche conducts an annual survey of holiday gift giving. According to their 2007 survey, respondents planned to purchase an average of twenty-three gifts for friends, family, and other acquaintances. Twenty-three gifts!?! It's hard enough to buy one thing for yourself. How on earth could givers figure out twenty-three things to get for others? If recent history is any guide, our gift spending will total roughly a few hundred billion dollars worldwide this year. At the same time, many good causes will go begging.

While it is hollow to suggest that we should give more carefully, at the same time the first step toward improvement is acknowledging that we have a problem. If you take the arguments in the book to mean—as I do—that we have a problem, then knowing this, you may seek betterment. Remember how Tommy (who wanted Grand Theft Auto IV but got a kaleidoscope) was too polite to tell his grandma she made a mistake? So she didn't know. Well, now she does.

134

135

My hope for change recalls the old lightbulb joke: "How many psychologists does it take to change a light bulb?" "Only one, but it has to *want* to change." Similarly, it takes only you to destroy less value at the holidays, but you have to be aware of your problem and want to change.

It's generally hard to change people's behavior. But one development that gives me hope is the rapid adoption of gift cards. They've gone from a blip to perhaps a third of holiday spending in a decade. They have shed the stigma of cash to become an acceptable—even highly sought-after—gift. While there are reasons for misgivings about gift cards—as I discussed above in chapter 12—their rapid adoption by givers and embrace by recipients give reason for hope that people are able to change their behavior to make their giving less destructive.

The idealized Christmas gift is a carefully chosen item that delights the recipient, opening his eyes to a new consumption possibility, and at the same time functions as a conduit of warm feeling between giver and recipient. Part of this tall order is delighting the recipient, meaning delivering him (or her) something that he would have loved to have, if only he had been aware of it. In short, the idealized gift actually beats cash.

Our gifts can sometimes beat cash, but this requires givers to know recipients well. Using intimate knowledge of their preferences and current possessions, along with your superior information about some products, you can sometimes find things that recipients would have been delighted to buy themselves, if only they had known about them. These are things like your obscure music discovery that you think—based on some experience—that I'd like, or that comic book you know has eluded me for twenty years. That is, we can try to give them things that they would immediately recognize that they want, but have been unaware of.

Givers know some of the recipients of those twenty-three gifts, close friends and immediate family, quite well. If you also see them frequently, you probably have a good idea about things they would like but do not already have. Buying specific noncash gifts for them, while not without risk, is not entirely hopeless. It's actually likely to generate reasonably high yields.

You know your young children as well—or better—than they know themselves, so you should keep giving them holiday gifts. They expect it, love it, and would be disappointed to lose it. Besides, their preferences are not specific enough for gifts to disappoint them much at Christmas.

You also know your close friends and other members of your immediate families well, so you should continue to buy them gifts when (a) you have a generous impulse and (b) you have some reason to chose what you are buying. Perhaps you stumbled across something that, with your intimate knowledge of that person's preferences, you bet would be great for him or her.

No matter how well you know your recipients, big-ticket items remain risky gift purchases. If surprising your recipient is not absolutely necessary, then there are some easy solutions, such as gift registries or wish lists. The way that universities and other nonprofit institutions solicit funds provides some guidance here.

Universities sell the right to name buildings, schools, and other tangible and intangible assets. My alma mater Brandeis University famously sells the right to donate each book in its library. At first blush this appears unseemly. After all, in many cases the buildings or schools or books already exist at the school, so the gift doesn't seem to create anything. Are these naming opportunities scams recalling entreaties like "Would you like to buy the Brooklyn Bridge?" Or are they mechanisms to ensure sensible resource use?

Donors to schools like to know they had a tangible impact on the school: for example, if their gift allows the construction of a new building adorned with their name. If they give the school unrestricted cash, it might end up financing something uninspiring, like faculty salaries.

One strategy would be for the school to let donors dictate the development of the school, based on what they want to give. But the school has a good idea of what it needs, whether a new stadium or a new art history building, and donor-led planning might result in more athletic or business school facilities than the university deems necessary. Another strategy is for the school to undertake the projects it finds useful, then to seek funding after the fact, through "naming opportunities," already-planned or completed projects available to be named for a person willing to pay a specified sum. At Lynchburg College, the stadium can be named Waldfogel Stadium if I pony up $2 million. The track is mine for $1 million. At MIT the opportunity to name an existing full professorship the "Waldfogel Chair" goes for $3 million. Viewed this way, these price tags on existing edifices are not unseemly at all. Rather, they reflect the school's coordination of financial support for its coherent investment decisions.

Can we use naming at Christmas? Yes, in a few ways. Suppose that, as spring arrives, a family decides to buy new bicycles. This can be a substantial expense, at least a few hundred dollars per bike plus a few hundred more for the car carrier. They've talked it over, and they know they want bikes, so this purchase will have high yield. They could wait for Christmas to buy the bikes and enjoy them a year from now. Or they could buy them now. A problem with spending the $2,000 now is that it makes it hard to afford the family's Christmas presents later.

But the family could buy the bikes and use them all year. Then, at Christmas, they could sell Santa the naming opportunity on the bike gift. This works for family vacations, boats, or whatever. The idea, in short, is to make Santa the benefactor of your good—and efficient—gift ideas. Gift registries, popular at weddings, accomplish the same thing. The bride and groom list the items they need, and wedding participants pay for the right to claim, say, the fourth place setting as their gift.

Another way for giving to beat cash is through paternalism, or salubrious gifts that protect our recipients from their mistakes. An extreme example illustrates the point. You don't want to give cash, or anything that can free up cash, to drug addicts because it will enable self-destructive consumption. Instead, you give them food or warm clothes. Most of our recipients, thankfully, are not drug addicts. But paternalistic giving can work in more ordinary contexts. Even in cold winter climates, the last thing most kids would buy with their own money is a hat. So a gift of a hat—provided it's not such an embarrassing hat that the kid is inclined to "lose" it immediately—makes the kid better off despite himself.

Kids and drug addicts are not the only ones making consumption mistakes. Economists are in widespread agreement that most people don't save enough because of shortcomings in decision making involving the distant future. A gift of future consumption—say, money available during retirement, thirty years hence—could make the recipient better off than anything you might give today. This approach requires selflessness, since by the time he realizes he's grateful, you may be long gone.

But what about the other recipients on your list? What about your boss, your employees, your out-of-town relatives, the hostess at a friend-of-a-friend's holiday party? You rarely, if ever, see these people and have no idea what they like, save, perhaps, for knowledge that Harold likes golf or Mildred needlepoint. You have virtually no chance of beating—or even coming near—cash by buying specific gifts for these people. And there's your scoundrel brother-in-law who blows all his money at the track, making you wonder if your little niece will get to go to college. Then there's your rich uncle who has refined tastes and already owns everything he wants. Buying him stuff is hopeless, and giving him cash is like hauling coals to Newcastle. What do you do for all those people?

Outside the intimate circle of the immediate family and close friends, you probably cannot find things delightful to the recipient that he could not himself find. You are unlikely to beat cash with the items you choose; your goal is instead to avoid destroying a lot of value. In short, your best hope is for your gift to be like cash. If the recipient is your niece or grandchild, custom

140

141

allows you to give cash directly. For many other arm's-length relationships requiring gifts, gift cards are a solution, particularly if—as I discuss below—retailers improve gift cards.

What if you have no idea what your recipient would like? And, related, what if your recipient already has everything he could want, because he's either rich or ascetic? What then? How about giving *through* your recipient, as between Buffett and Gates? Even if your recipient is richer than you, a dollar given to charity *through* him can raise well-being because the coals bypass Newcastle.

I have two ideas that harness the impulse to give Christmas gifts as a force for good. The first is charity gift cards. On what other luxuries, besides retirement savings, do high-income individuals spend a bigger share of their income? Cash contributions to charity. This means that the rest of us would like to give more to charity, if only we had the money. The obvious solution: giving people money that they can use only for making charitable contributions.

Gifts to charity offer a double dividend. First—again—it appears that people would like to give more to charity if their incomes allowed. Second, when done right, charities allocate resources to activities with high social return. If a dollar invested in mosquito netting in Africa prevents five dollars' worth of disease, that's a 500 percent yield, which is a far cry from the typical recipient valuation per dollar of gift spending.

In the past few years, a number of organizations (such as Charity Navigator and charitygift certificates.org) have appeared offering just this service, in the form of charity gift cards. A giver goes to a Web site and purchases a gift card that allows the recipient to designate which charity receives the money.

Charity Navigator is like a Consumer Reports of charities, evaluating the effectiveness of a large number of charities using their tax disclosure documents. Since November 2007, the organization has also offered the "Good Card," "a gift card for charity where the recipients get to donate to their charity of choice. Your friends, family and colleagues all have their favorite charities and by purchasing a Good Card you can give them the perfect gift to celebrate the holidays, birthdays, graduations and other momentous occasions."

As with many other gifts, charity gift cards, like cheese, have the capacity to be turned into cash. If the recipient had already planned $500 in charitable donations this year and then, on receiving a $100 charity gift card, reduces her own contribution to $400, then this gift is effectively a $100 cash gift to your recipient. But even if your recipient goes the tacky route and cashes out, your gift will still produce more satisfaction than a typical noncash gift.

My second idea is to fix gift cards to make them more effective, ideally with charities as the beneficiaries. When a giver buys a gift card, she should be confident that the value of the card will increase the satisfaction of someone she cares about. Given that about 10 percent of gift card value is never redeemed by recipients, givers cannot have the confidence they seek. And because gift card recipients are human—meaning harried and disorganized—it's unlikely that recipient behavior can solve this problem. What's needed is a card that, by prior agreement, transfers unused card balances to designated good causes.

So I propose that stores issue gift cards that expire after, say, twelve or eighteen months. And at expiration, the remaining balance is given to charity. Indeed, the charity could be chosen by the giver, and it might be right on the card (imagine a Gap gift card co-branded with, say, CARE). Maybe the theme is "keep the change," meaning that when you buy a $25 shirt on your $30 card, you tell the Gap to "keep the change" for CARE. Perhaps the Gap could issue a CARE receipt so that itemizing taxpayers could deduct their contribution.

Given the volume of unredeemed gift cards, I'm guessing that good causes could pick up a billion per year through this mechanism if a few socially conscious retailers—the Gap, Target, Wal-Mart, Macy's—got on board.

The selfish analogue to the above is gift cards that are redeemable for cash. One reason gift card balances end up in limbo is that the recipient has no interest in the store. Or maybe she spent $20 of the $25 balance. There's nothing available for $5 that interests her, and she doesn't want to contribute her own money. California legislators passed a law effective January 2008 that compels retailers to redeem gift card balances for cash when the remaining balance falls below $10.

Worldwide, we're spending a few hundred billion dollars per year on the holidays. In the process, we're destroying $25 billion annually. It is unrealistic to expect us to forgo Christmas and instead use the billions the West spent at the mall on charity. But if we gave more carefully and, where appropriate, channeled some of the giving to good causes through our friends, we could realistically expect to reduce the waste from ill-chosen gifts and, beyond that, to raise some money for good causes. Perhaps we can raise a few hundred million or even a billion. If we can do this together, maybe I can join the ranks of jet-setting do-gooder economists who get to hang with Bono.

A specter has been haunting the rich economies of the West, and that specter is wasteful gift giving. Gift givers of the world unite. You have nothing to lose but deadweight loss and a world of satisfaction to gain.

Notes

Notes to Chapter II
Spending and Satisfaction

7–8 George W. Bush's statements on shopping appear in his September 20, 2001, Address to a Joint Session of Congress and the American People (http://www.whitehouse.gov/news/releases/2001/09/20010920-8.html, accessed August 15, 2008), as well as a December 20, 2006, press conference (http://www.whitehouse.gov/news/releases/2006/12/20061220-1.html, accessed August 15, 2008).

16 Many of the lessons of behavioral economics are readably recounted in Dan Ariely, *Predictably Irrational* (New York: Harper Collins, 2008).

17 Information on the disappointment consumers experience after purchasing music CDs is presented in Rafael Rob and Joel Waldfogel,

"Piracy on the High C's," *Journal of Law and Economics* 49 (2006): 29–62.

Notes to Chapter III
U.S. Holiday Spending

23 The NRF holiday-spending definition, along with their forecast of 2007 holiday spending, appears in "Citing Economic Concerns, NRF Forecasts Holiday Sales Gains of Four Percent," September 20, 2007, at www.nrf.com, accessed September 26, 2007.

24 Economic studies of seasonality include Robert B. Barsky and Jeffrey A. Miron, "The Seasonal Cycle and the Business Cycle," *Journal of Political Economy*. 97, no. 3 (1989): 503–34. Data on monthly U.S. retail sales are available from the Census Bureau, in "Monthly Retail Trade and Food Services," http://www.census .gov/mrts/www/mrts.html, accessed August 4, 2008.

26 A number of polling organizations provide annual surveys of holiday-spending plans. See http://www.gallup.com/poll/25495/Christmas-Shoppers-Appear-Jolly-Mood.aspx, accessed September 13, 2008, for Gallup Results. See "Consumers in a Festive Mood as the Holiday Season Approaches, The Conference Board

Reports," November 20, 2007, at http://www
.conference-board.org/cgi-bin/MsmGo.exe?
grab_id=0&EXTRA_ARG=&host_id=42&page
_id=256&query=christmas&hiword=CHRIST
MAN%20christmas%20, accessed September
13, 2008.

26– We use estimates of the number of households
27   in the United States from the Census Bureau
      (http://www.census.gov/population/projections/
      nation/hh-fam/table1n.txt), translating the sur-
      vey averages into national numbers.

28   See   http://www.americansportscastersonline
      .com/wolfinterview.html,   accessed   July   28,
      2008, for information about Warner Wolfe and
      his "let's go to the video" catchphrase.

148

149

Notes to Chapter IV
How Much Waste Occurs at Christmas?

29   The Citizens Against Government Waste's an-
      nual "Pig Books" are available at http://www
      .cagw.org/.

32   The *New York Times* reported on the *Chicago
      Tribune*'s editorial in Hubert Herring, "Dislike
      Those Suspenders? Don't Complain, Quanti-
      fy!" *New York Times*, December 25, 1994.

32   Academic studies responding to my initial pa-

per include, for example, John A. List and Jason F. Shogren, "The Deadweight Loss of Christmas: Comment," *American Economic Review* 88 (1998): 1350–55; Bradley J. Ruffle and Orit Tykocinski, "The Deadweight Loss of Christmas: Comment," *American Economic Review* 90 (2000): 319–24; Sara J. Solnick and David Hemenway, "The Deadweight Loss of Christmas: Comment," *American Economic Review* 86 (1996): 1299–1305.

33– The estimates of the deadweight loss of Christ-
34 mas based on comparisons of the yield on gifts and people's own purchases are presented in Joel Waldfogel, "Does Consumer Irrationality Trump Consumer Sovereignty?" *Review of Economics and Statistics* 87, no. 4 (2005): 691–96.

36 Results on how the efficiency of giving varies with the frequency of contact between giver and recipients are described in Joel Waldfogel, "Gifts, Cash, and Stigma," *Economic Inquiry* 40 (2002): 415–27.

37– The American Time Use Survey is available at
38 http://www.bls.gov/tus/. The time allocations for 2007 are reported in table A-1, "Time Spent in Detailed Primary Activities" (http://www.bls.gov/tus/tables/a1_2007.pdf).

39 Sources documenting shortcomings of decision making warranting paternalistic interventions include Daniel Kahneman, "New Challenges to the Rationality Assumption," *Journal of Institutional and Theoretical Economics* 150, no. 1 (1994): 18–36; and Richard H. Thaler and Cass R. Sunstein, *Nudge: Improving Decisions about Health, Wealth, and Happiness* (New Haven: Yale University Press, 2008).

40 Arthur Okun introduced the leaky bucket metaphor in *Equality and Efficiency: The Big Tradeoff* (Washington, DC: The Brookings Institution, 1975).

Notes to Chapter V
Why We Do It: Are Gift Recipients Crackheads, or What?

Some observers emphasize additional motives for gift giving beyond those I focus on, such as the imposition of reciprocal obligations. I give to you today so that you are obliged to reciprocate in the future, which may be handy if my crops fail. This explanation was articulated by Marcel Mauss in *The Gift* (first published in Paris in 1925), based on descriptions of tribal preindustrial societies, and, while fascinating, seems distant from contemporary holiday giving in advanced Western countries.

41 The suggestion that government grants of cheese are sometimes cash stems from the fact that the U.S. government sometimes makes gifts of cheese. For a description of the USDA commodity giveaways, see Michael Lipsky and Marc A. Thibodeau, "Feeding the Hungry with Surplus Commodities," *Political Science Quarterly* 103, no. 2 (Summer 1988): 223–44.

42 Some information on the size of the federal portion of the U.S. public housing budget is available in "Bush Administration Seeks $38.5 Billion HUD Budget in 2009: *Additional $1 Billion Requested for Housing Counseling, Affordable Housing & Homeless*" (http://www.hud.gov/news/release.cfm?content=pro8-014.cfm, accessed September 13, 2008).

42 Data on U.S. spending on education are drawn from National Center for Education Statistics Fast Facts, at http://nces.ed.gov/fastfacts/display.asp?id=372, accessed September 13, 2008.

54–55 Data on the role of gifts in income are available in the Consumer Expenditure Survey, at http://www.bls.gov/cex/, accessed August 4, 2008. See the tables http://www.bls.gov/cex/2006/Standard/income.pdf and http://www.bls.gov/cex/2006/Standard/higherincome.pdf, accessed September 13, 2008.

Notes to Chapter VI
Giving and Waste around the World

57 U.S. and world population are from http://www
    .census.gov/main/www/popclock.html. U.S.
    share of world gasoline consumption is from
    http://www.nrdc.org/air/energy/fensec.asp, both
    accessed August 3, 2008.

57 See the obesity statistics at http://www.heart
    stats.org/temp/Figsp11.14hspweb07.xls, ac-
    cessed July 31, 2008.

58 The OECD retail sales data for many coun-
    tries are available at their Main Economic
    Indicators site: http://oecd-stats.ingenta.com/
    OECD/TableViewer/DimView.aspx?TableNa
    me=6jmeicd.ivt&IF_Language=eng, accessed
    August 8, 2008. While the OECD has some
    Israeli data, the monthly retail sales data for
    Israel were obtained from the Bank of Israel
    site: http://www.bankisrael.gov.il/series/en/cat
    alog/commerce/value%20of%20sales%20indi
    ces/, accessed August 8, 2008.

59 Specifically, we calculate our basic measure of
    the Yuletide spending bump as follows: if
    r(month) is the retail sales index in any given
    month and R is the actual value of retail sales
    for the year, then the Christmas share of the
    year's retail sales can be calculated as

$$\{r(dec) - 0.5[r(nov) + r(jan)]\}/R,$$

where *"jan"* is the January immediately following the December in *"dec."*

60 Data on the Christian share of nations' population are drawn from Cross-National Data: Religion Indexes, Religious Adherents, and Other Data, The Association of Religious Data Archives, http://thearda.com/Archive/CrossNational.asp.

61 Information on Russian Christmas is drawn from "Christmas Had to Survive Dark Years of Communism to Return to Russia," *Pravda*, December 12, 2007 (http://english.pravda.ru/russia/history/25-12-2007/103134-christmas-0, accessed August 8, 2008), as well as Alessandra Stanley, "Dec. 25 in Russia: The Adoration of the Monetary," *New York Times*, December 24, 1996.

61– Information on Japan's Christmas traditions
62 is drawn from "Christmas in Japan," http://www.japaneselifestyle.com.au/culture/christmas.html, accessed September 26, 2007, and another document also entitled "Christmas in Japan," http://www.rochedalss.eq.edu.au/xmas/japanchristmas.htm, accessed September 26, 2007.

62 Information on the customary gift giving holidays in Israel is provided in http://israeltrade
.gov.il/NR/rdonlyres/4015696D-CEB6-4544-
B9FF-DA95338749B1/0/TheGiftGivingSeasons
.pdf.

65 The Euromonitor data on retail sales by country are available at http://www.euromonitor
.com/, accessed August 11, 2008.

67 Friends and acquaintances who administered
the survey in various countries include Helen
Weeds (Warwick, UK), Johan Stennek (Gote-
borg, Sweden), Frank Verboven (Leuven,
Belgium), Pedro Garcia (Brazil), Fabrizio   154
Germano (Spain), and Stefan Behringer (Germany).   155

68– The study of Indian gift giving is Parag Waknis
69   and Ajit Gaikwad, "The Deadweight Loss of
     Diwali" (working paper, Kohinoor Business
     School, February 2006).

Notes to Chapter VII
A Century of American Yuletide Spending

Readers interested in the history of Christmas in
the United States should see Stephen Nissenbaum,
The Battle for Christmas: A Cultural History of

America's Most Cherished Holiday (New York: Vintage, 1997).

72 Monthly retail sales data for the United States are available back to 1967 at http://www.census.gov/mrts/www/noverview.html, accessed July 28, 2008. Historical retail sales figures for the United States can be found in, among other places, the monthly U.S. Department of Commerce's Survey of Current Business, which is available in an excellent electronic archive provided by the St. Louis Federal Reserve Bank in its Federal Reserve Archive System for Economic Research (FRASER) project: http://fraser.stlouisfed.org/publications/SCB/pageinventory/, accessed July 28, 2008.

73 While the Yuletide spending bump has been relatively constant since 1935, it has been declining relative to January since the mid-1990s because of gift card redemption. We return to this topic in chapter 12.

74 Historical dollar figures are translated to current dollar amounts with the CPI calculator: http://www.bls.gov/data/inflation_calculator.htm.

75 Lyrics for "The Wells Fargo Wagon" are available at http://www.stlyrics.com/lyrics/themusic

man/wellsfargowagon.htm, accessed July 28, 2008.

77 Harriet Beecher Stowe's prescient observations on Christmas are quoted in Beth Teitell, "It's the Receipt That Counts," *Boston Globe*, November 25, 2007.

Notes to Chapter VIII
Have Yourself a Borrowed Little Christmas

78– Wal-Mart announced the end of its layaway
79 program in a September 2006 news release, http://walmartstores.com/FactsNews/News Room/5923.aspx, accessed August 29, 2008.

79 The contemporary scholarly account of Christmas clubs, Lloyd M. Cosgrove, "Christmas Clubs," *Quarterly Journal of Economics* 41, no. 4 (August 1927): 732–39, is the source for the quotes.

80 The Christmas club deposit data are available in Board of Governors of the Federal Reserve System (U.S.), Annual Statistical Digest, Banking and Monetary Statistics 1914–1941, table 21, page 78. Available at http://fraser.stlouisfed .org/publications/bms, accessed May 19, 2009.

81 Data on the volume of credit outstanding are drawn from the U.S. Federal Reserve Bank's

156

157

"G19" "Consumer Credit" series, available at http://www.federalreserve.gov/releases/g19/Current/.

84 U.S. debts to foreigners, in the form of international holdings of Treasury securities, are reported at http://www.ustreas.gov/tic/mfh.txt, which provides a breakdown of foreign ownership of U.S. Treasury securities in 2008.

87 The script containing Homer Simpson's line is available at http://www.geocities.com/great_tv_quotes/shows/simpsons.html, accessed September 15, 2008.

88 The 7,300 percent interest rate on payday loans is derived $1.18^{26} - 1$. See Paige Marta Skiba and Jeremy Tobacman, "Payday Loans, Uncertainty, and Discounting: Explaining Patterns of Borrowing, Repayment, and Default" (unpublished manuscript, August 2008), at http://bpp.wharton.upenn.edu/tobacman/papers/payday.pdf, accessed September 15, 2008.

Notes to Chapter IX
Is Christmas Like Spam, Underwear,
or Caviar?

92 The National Income and Product Account Handbook, http://www.bea.gov/national/pdf/NIPAhandbookch1-4.pdf, p. 2-8 (accessed Au-

gust 15, 2008), provides background on the NIPA data.

94 Data on the share of low-income households' expenditures on food and housing are drawn from table 46, "Income before Taxes: Shares of Average Annual Expenditures and Sources of Income," Consumer Expenditure Survey, 2006, http://www.bls.gov/cex/2006/share/income .pdf. Data on high-income consumers' expenditures are drawn from table 2301, "Higher Income before Taxes: Shares of Average Annual Expenditures and Sources of Income," Consumer Expenditure Survey, 2006, http:// www.bls.gov/cex/2006/share/higherincome.pdf. 158

94 Health care is wildly different, however. The 159 over-time data indicate that as we've gotten richer, we spend a bigger share of our resources on health care. The cross-household data indicate that today higher-income people do not devote a larger share of their expenditure to health care than do lower-income people. These two findings are not necessarily inconsistent. They mean that people of all income levels consume more health care now than they did three generations ago. The striking difference between the health care income elasticity in cross-sectional and time series data has been noted elsewhere; see Thomas

Getzen, "Health Care Is an Individual Necessity and a National Luxury" (working paper, Temple University, 2008).

95 The Gallup Poll cited in the chapter is available at http://www.gallup.com/poll/102865/ Christmas-Spending-Projection-Still-Looks-Positive.aspx#2, accessed September 9, 2008.

96 Cell midpoints for the elasticity calculations based on the Gallup numbers are $15,000, $53,000, and $100,000 for income levels and $125, $375, $750, and $1,250 for spending levels.

96 The Siena and Conference Board surveys are available at http://www.siena.edu/uploaded Files/Home/Parents_and_Community/Com munity_Page/Siena_Research_Institute/Freq %20and%20Cross%20Tab.pdf and http://www .conference-board.org/cgi-bin/MsmGo.exe? grab_id=0&EXTRA_ARG=&SCOPE=Public &host_id=42&page_id=223&query=holiday %20gift%20giving&hiword=gift%20GIFTED %20giving%20HOLIDAYS%20oholiday%20 GIFTS%20 and http://www.conference-board .org/pdf_free/Spending2007.pdf, respectively, both accessed September 9, 2008.

97 Expenditure data on cash contributions are

drawn from http://www.bls.gov/cex/csxgloss
.htm#otherx, accessed July 30, 2008.

Notes to Chapter X
Christmas and Commercialism:
Are Santa and Jesus on the Same Team?
If So, Who's Team Captain?

99   Art Conrad's story is documented in Susan Gil-
     more, "Newcomer on Block Calls Santa Dis-
     play Art, but Bremerton Neighbors Repulsed,"
     Seattle Times, December 23, 2007, accessed at
     http://community.seattletimes.nwsource.com/
     archive/?date=20071223&slug=santa23m, July
     21, 2008.

99   Information about the pope's 2005 condemna-
     tion of commercialism is drawn from the
     Catholic News Agency press release "Pope
     Encourages Family Nativity Scenes, Con-
     demns Christmas Commercialism," Vatican
     City, December 12, 2005 (www.catholicnews
     agency.com).

100 The New American Dream organization's ex-
     hortation to "Simplify the Holidays" is online
     at http://www.newdream.org/holiday/index.php,
     accessed July 28, 2008.

101 Information about Crown Financial Ministries is available at www.crown.org/aboutcrown and in Howard Dayton, "Countering the Commercialization of Christmas" (Baptist Press), http://www.crosswalk.com/finances/1449409/, accessed July 27, 2008.

102 The American Family Association's mission is available at http://www.afa.net/mission.asp, accessed August 11, 2008.

102– Fox anchor Bill O'Reilly's views on Christ-
103 mas are presented in "Christmas Under Siege: The Big Picture," December 24, 2004, at http://www.foxnews.com/story/0,2933,140742, 00.html, accessed August 11, 2008. I have drawn on the observations of Adam Cohen, "Editorial Observer; This Season's War Cry: Commercialize Christmas, or Else," *New York Times*, December 25, 2005.

Notes to Chapter XI
Stop Carping; It's All for the Best

107– My references to the norms associated with
108   polite table manners are drawn from Norbert Elias's account of the rise of the fork. See Johan Goudsblom and Stephen Mennell, *The Norbert Elias Reader* (Oxford: Blackwell, 1997).

109 The Wikipedia entry http://en.wikipedia.org/ wiki/The_Jetsons provides a sufficiently authoritative description of the Hanna-Barbera cartoon *The Jetsons*. Preston McAfee's *Introduction to Economic Analysis* (2006), a free online microeconomics textbook, provides an even more authoritative description of principal-agent models, at http://www.introecon .com/.

111 See the Grand Theft Auto IV Web site, at http://www.rockstargames.com/IV/, for a description of the game. But only after you claim to be old enough. When I sought to enter the site claiming I was born in 2001, my University of Pennsylvania office computer was permanently locked out: "Sorry, you may not view this site." The site was accessed August 6, 2008.

Notes to Chapter XII
Making Giving More Efficient with Cash
and Gift Cards

114 For a nice, and perhaps the only, scholarly account of gift cards, see Jennifer Pate Offenberg, "Gift Cards," *Journal of Economic Perspectives* 21, no. 2 (Spring 2007): 227–38.

114 Quotes on the diminishing stigma of gift cards
     are drawn from National Public Radio, *All
     Things Considered*, "Sales of Gift Cards Grow,
     and Transpire Earlier," December 13, 2006, at
     http://nl.newsbank.com/; Patrick Huguenin,
     Eloise Parker, and Jane Ridley, "The Present
     That They Really Want: Holiday Gift Cards,"
     New York Daily News, December 3, 2007;
     Kate Prahlad, "Merry Halloween! Christmas
     Shopping Now Starts Well before Thanksgiv-
     ing," *Southern Maryland Online*, November
     23, 2007 (at http://somd.com/news/headlines/
     2007/6773.shtml, accessed August 10, 2008).

114 Information on the desirability of gift cards to
     recipients is drawn from Huguenin, Parker,
     and Ridley (2007), cited above, and Judy Lin.
     "It's the Law: On Balance, Card Recipients
     Will Get Break," *Sacramento Bee*, December
     25, 2007.

115 For information on the treatment of gift cards
     in U.S. retail sales statistics, see "Monthly Re-
     tail Trade Survey, Frequently Asked Ques-
     tions," http://www.census.gov/mrts/www/faq
     .html. "Question: Are gift certificates included
     in retail sales estimates? Answer: Yes. Accord-
     ing to generally accepted accounting princi-
     ples, sales from gift certificates are included in

the retail sales of firms at the time the gift certificate is redeemed."

115– Lorrie Grant, "January Evolves into a Hot
116 Month for Retail Sales," *USA Today*, January
22, 2006, provides information on January gift
card redemption and the "hot month for retail" quote.

116 The retail sales data changed from SIC codes
to NAICS codes, and the old series was dis-
continued in 2000. The new series begins in
1992, and the overlap shows that the series are
very similar, so the recent years of the new series can be viewed as a continuation of the
old.

116 Data on gift card nonredemption are drawn
from the Montgomery County, MD, Office of
Consumer Protection, "Gift Cards 2007: Best
and Worst Retail Cards; A Deeper View of
Bank Cards Doesn't Improve Their Look,"
http://www.montgomerycountymd.gov/content/
ocp/giftcards2007final.pdf, as well as earlier
annual reports.

117 Information on nonredemption in this chapter
is drawn from Mark Clothier, "Retailers Find
Profit Windfall—Unused Gift Cards," *Bloom-
berg News*, February 27, 2006 (http://seattlepi

.nwsource.com/business/260931_giftcards27
.html, accessed August 10, 2008).

118 The *CFO Magazine* quotes are drawn from
Alan Rappeport, "Re-Gifting: Unused Gift
Cards Can Boost Company Income; As Black
Friday approaches, people will be spending
billions on gift cards. Many companies will
profit from those who lose them," CFO.com,
November 21, 2007.

118 For information on the laws surrounding gift
cards, see Daniel R. Horne, "Gift Cards: Disclosure One Step Removed," *Journal of Consumer Affairs* 41, no. 2 (Winter 2007): 341–50;
and Charles Owen Kile, Jr., "Accounting for
Gift Cards," *Journal of Accountancy*, November 2007 (www.journalofaccountancy.com/Is
sues/2007/Nov/AccountingForGiftCards.htm,
accessed February 2, 2009).

Notes to Chapter XIII
Giving and Redistribution

122 Ted Turner's gift was documented in "Ted
Turner Donates $1 Billion to 'U.N. Causes,'"
CNN.com, September 19, 1997 (at http://edi
tion.cnn.com/US/9709/18/turner.gift/).

123 Information on the Gates Foundation is avail-

able in "Foundation Timeline," at http://www
.gatesfoundation.org/about/Pages/foundation-
timeline.aspx, accessed November 18, 2008.

124 The Cato Institute perspective is available in
James A. Dorn, "Ending Tax Socialism," *Cato.
org*, September 13, 1996, http://www.cato.org/
pub_display.php?pub_id=6297, accessed August 26, 2008.

125 Information on marginal tax rates in the United States is obtained from the Congressional
Budget Office report "Effective Marginal Tax
Rates on Labor Income," November 2005
(http://www.cbo.gov/ftpdocs/68xx/doc6854/11-
10-LaborTaxation.pdf, accessed August 26,
2008), as well as from Emmanuel Saez, "Reported Incomes and Marginal Tax Rates,
1960–2000: Evidence and Policy Implications"
(NBER Working Paper 10273, January 2004),
at http://www.nber.org/papers/w10273.

127– See William Easterly, *The White Man's Bur-
128 den: Why the West's Efforts to Aid the Rest
Have Done So Much Ill and So Little Good*
(New York: Penguin Press, 2006), for a pessi-
mistic view on development policy. See Jeffrey
Sachs, *The End of Poverty* (New York: Penguin Press, 2005), for a more optimistic view.

128 Recommendations of the Copenhagen Con-

sensus are available in a ranked list of solutions at http://www.copenhagenconsensus.com/Default.aspx?ID=953, accessed November 18, 2008. The quote is drawn from "The Basic Idea," at http://www.copenhagenconsensus.com/Default.aspx?ID=1014, accessed August 25, 2008.

129 The cost-benefit results are presented in "Results of Copenhagen Consensus, 2008," at http://www.copenhagenconsensus.com/Default.aspx?ID=956, accessed August 25, 2008.

130 Data from the National Center for Charitable Statistics are available at http://nccsdataweb.urban.org/NCCS/Public/index.php, accessed August 25, 2008.

130 Data on total private U.S. giving are drawn from "Charitable Giving: Statistics and Trends," http://www.generousgiving.org/page.asp?sec=4&page=161#45, accessed August 25, 2008.

130– International foreign aid comparisons are
131 drawn from the OECD Statistical Annex of the 2007 Development Co-operation Report, at http://www.oecd.org/document/9/0,3343,en_2649_34485_1893129_1_1_1_1,00.html, accessed August 26, 2008.

132– The story of Buffett's gift through Gates is re-
133 counted in Carol J. Loomis, "Warren Buffett
Gives It Away." *Fortune*, July 10, 2006, 57.

*Notes to Chapter XIV
Solutions—Making Gift Giving
a Force for Good*

135 Results of the Deloitte Touche survey for 2007
are reported in "Deloitte 2007 Annual Holiday Survey," at http://public.deloitte.com/me
dia/0001/US_2007_Holiday_spending.pdf.

139 Prices of naming opportunities were glimpsed
at Lynchburg's "Naming Opportunities" (http://
www.lynchburg.edu/namingopps.xml, accessed
August 20, 2008) and MIT's "Naming Opportunities List" (http://giving.mit.edu/ways/nam
ing/list.html#scholarships, accessed August 20,
2008).

143 Information on Charity Navigator and charity-
giftcertificates.org is available at http://www
.charitynavigator.org/ and http://charitygiftcer
tificates.org, respectively. For information on
the Good Card, see Alan Kraus, "Gift Cards
Go Philanthropic," *New York Times*, December 5, 2007, at http://www.nytimes.com/2007/
12/05/technology/techspecial2/05card.html.

168

169

Index

INDEX